WITHDRAWN FROM HAVERING COLLEGES
SIXTH FORM LIBRARY

Mussolini and Fascist Italy

'An excellent introduction to one of the most contentious issues of modern European history' *British Book News*

'The best short introduction to Italian Fascism' *Philip Morgan, University of Hull*

In *Mussolini and Fascist Italy* Martin Blinkhorn explains the significance of the man, the movement and the regime which dominated Italian life between 1922 and the closing stages of the Second World War.

He examines:

- those aspects of post-Risorgimento Italy which provided the long-term context vital to an understanding of Fascism
- the social and political convulsions wrought by economic change after 1890 and by Italy's intervention in the First World War
- the Fascist movement's rapid rise from obscurity to power and the subsequent establishment of Mussolini's dictatorship
- the history of the Fascist regime until its demise during the Second World War
- the ways in which Italian Fascism has been understood by contemporary analysts and by historians

The third edition of this best-selling *Lancaster Pamphlet* provides an expanded and fully updated analysis. New features include additional material on Fascist totalitarianism and a completely revised consideration of the ways in which Fascism has been interpreted.

Martin Blinkhorn is Professor of Modern European History at Lancaster University. His publications on Fascism include *Fascists and Conservatives* (Routledge, 1990) and *Fascism and the Right in Europe, 1919–1945* (2000).

IN THE SAME SERIES

General Editors: Eric J. Evans and P. D. King

LANCASTER PAMPHLETS

Mussolini and Fascist Italy

Third Edition

Martin Blinkhorn

Routledge
Taylor & Francis Group

LONDON AND NEW YORK

First published 1984
by Methuen & Co. Ltd
Reprinted 1987

Reprinted 1989, 1990, 1991
by Routledge
2 Park Square, Milton Park, Abingdon, Oxon OX14 4RN

Second edition published 1994

Reprinted 2003, 2005

Third edition 2006

Simultaneously published in the USA and Canada
by Routledge
270 Madison Ave, New York, NY 10016

Routledge is an imprint of the Taylor & Francis Group, an informa business

© 1984, 1994, 2006 Martin Blinkhorn

Typeset in Bembo by RefineCatch Limited, Bungay, Suffolk
Printed and bound in Great Britain by TJ International Ltd, Padstow, Cornwall

All rights reserved. No part of this book may be reprinted or
reproduced or utilised in any form or by any electronic, mechanical,
or other means, now known or hereafter invented, including
photocopying and recording, or in any information storage or
retrieval system, without permission in writing from the publishers.

British Library Cataloguing in Publication Data
A catalogue record for this book is available from the British Library

Library of Congress Cataloging in Publication Data
Blinkhorn, Martin, 1941–
Mussolini and fascist Italy / Martin Blinkhorn. – 3rd ed.
p. cm. – (Lancaster pamphlets)
Includes bibliographical references.
ISBN 0–415–26206–2 (hardback) – ISBN 0–415–26207–0 (pbk.) 1. Fascism—
Italy—History—20th century. 2. Mussolini, Benito, 1883–
1945. 3. Italy—Politics and government—1922–1945. I. Title. II. Series.
DG571.B54 2006
945.091—dc22

2006010092

ISBN10: 0-415-26206-2 (hbk)
ISBN10: 0-415-26207-0 (pbk)
ISBN10: 0-203-96926-X (ebk)

ISBN13: 978-0-415-26206-4 (hbk)
ISBN13: 978-0-415-26207-1 (pbk)
ISBN13: 978-0-203-96926-7 (ebk)

Contents

Foreword

The Lancaster Pamphlets series presents up-to-date, concise accounts and interpretations of major historical topics. The books span all periods from the ancient world to the late twentieth century. They are of particular value to those wanting to get an accessible overview of themes relevant to courses in universities and in other institutions of further and higher education. They can also be used with confidence by students preparing for AS and A2 examinations. Without being all-embracing, they bring the key themes and problems confronting students into sharper focus than the textbook writer can usually do. They explicitly provide the reader with the results of recent research which, again, the textbook may not provide. Since they are written by practising professional historians, they also convey individuality of approach as well as a synthesis of existing ideas. Above all, each volume in the Lancaster Pamphlets series gives readers an understanding of a topic sufficient to imbue confidence and, thereby, enthusiasm to move on to more detailed study if required.

Time chart

Before 1900

1859–70	Unification of Italy
1881	Electoral reform extends franchise to 2 million
1881–2	Italian ambitions in Egypt and Tunis thwarted
1883	Mussolini born at Predappio
1885–9	Italy occupies Eritrea and Somaliland
1892	Foundation of Italian Socialist Party (PSI)
1896	Italy defeated at Adowa
1898–1900	Period of socio-political crisis

1900–15

1902–4	Mussolini in Switzerland
1903–5	Giolitti's second administration
1904–6	Mussolini's military service
1906–9	Giolitti's third administration
1906–7	Mussolini teaching
1908	Mussolini begins journalistic career
	Revolutionary syndicalists leave PSI
1909	Mussolini in Trent
1910	Foundation of Italian Nationalist Association
1910–12	Mussolini in Forli

1911–12	Libyan war – opposed by Mussolini
1912	Left takes over PSI
	Mussolini editor of *Avanti*
	Giolitti's electoral reform – franchise extended to almost 9 million
1913	General election – Catholic and PSI advance
1914–15	Interventionist crisis
1914	Outbreak of war (August)
	Foundation of *Fasci di Azione Rivoluzionaria* (October)
	Mussolini leaves *Avanti*, founds *Il Popolo d'Italia* and is expelled from PSI (November–December)
1915	Treaty of London and Italian entry into war (April–May)

1915–24

1915–17	Mussolini on war service
1917	Caporetto – Italian defeat
1918	Vittorio Veneto – Italian victory
1918–20	*Biennio rosso* – 'two red years'
1919	*Fascio di Combattimento* founded (March)
	D'Annunzio seizes Fiume (September)
	General Election (November) – fascist failure, PSI and *popolari* become major parties
1920–2	Rise of fascism as mass movement
1920	Occupation of factories (August)
	D'Annunzio expelled from Fiume (December)
1921	General Election (May) – thirty-five fascists elected
	Abortive Pact of Pacification between fascists and socialists (summer)
	Foundation of PNF – fascism becomes a political party (November)
1922	Election of Pope Pius XI (February)
	Facta becomes prime minister (February)
	Unsuccessful socialist general strike (August)
	March on Rome – Mussolini becomes prime minister (October)
	Fascist Grand Council created (December)
1923	Nationalists join PNF (February)

	Electoral law revised
	Corfu affair (September)
	Chigi Palace Pact (December)
	Fascist militia created (December)
1923–4	Italy obtains Fiume
1924	General Election (April) under revised system – Fascist victory
	Matteotti affair (June–August) – secession of opposition from parliament
	Revolt of the consuls (December)

1925–45

1925–6	Legal and institutional basis of dictatorship created
1925	Mussolini announces dictatorship (January)
	Farinacci PNF secretary (January)
	Vidoni Palace pact (October)
1926	Turati replaces Farinacci as PNF secretary (April)
	Rocco's labour relations law
	Ministry of Corporations created
	Albanian protectorate declared
1927	Labour Charter published 'Quota 90'
1928	Fascist Labour Confederation split up
	Treaty of 'friendship' with Ethiopia
1929	Lateran Accords between Italy and papacy
	Grandi becomes foreign secretary
1930	Giuriati replaces Turati as PNF secretary
	Bottai becomes minister for Corporations
1931	Starace becomes PNF secretary
1932	Mussolini resumes foreign secretaryship
1933	IRI founded
1934	Mixed corporations created
	Austrian crisis – Italian troops sent to border (July)
	Incident on Ethiopia–Somaliland border (December)
1935	Stresa conference (April)
	Outbreak of Ethiopian war (October)
1936	End of Ethiopian war (May)
	Ciano becomes foreign secretary (June)

	Outbreak of Spanish Civil War – Italy intervenes (July)
	Formation of German–Italian Axis (October)
1938	German–Austrian *Anschluss* (union)
	Racial laws enacted
	Munich agreement (September)
1939	Chamber of Fasces and Corporations instituted
	Italy annexes Albania (April)
	Pact of Steel (May)
	Outbreak of war – Italy remains neutral (September)
1940	Italy enters war (June)
	Unsuccessful Italian invasion of Greece (October)
1941	Loss of Italian East Africa
	Italy joins German invasion of USSR and declares war on USA
1942	El Alamein
	Allies invade French North Africa
1943	Axis defeat in North Africa
	Strikes in northern Italy (March)
	Mussolini dismisses leading Fascists (February–April)
	Allies invade Sicily (July)
	Fascist Grand Council meeting – Mussolini deposed (24–25 July)
	Italian surrender (8 September)
	Mussolini rescued from Gran Sasso (12 September)
	Italy declares war on Germany (October)
	Congress of Verona (November)
1944–5	Allied advance through Italy
1945	Death of Mussolini (28 April)

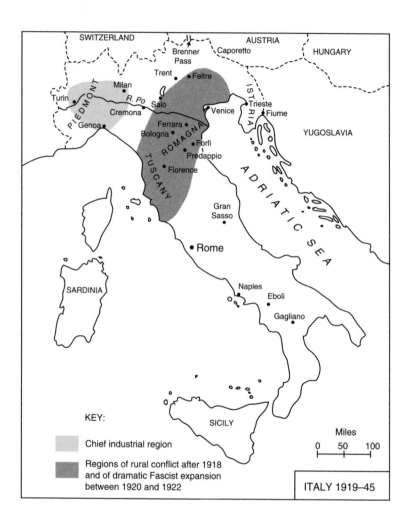

KEY:

Chief industrial region

Regions of rural conflict after 1918
and of dramatic Fascist expansion
between 1920 and 1922

Miles

0   50   100

ITALY 1919–45

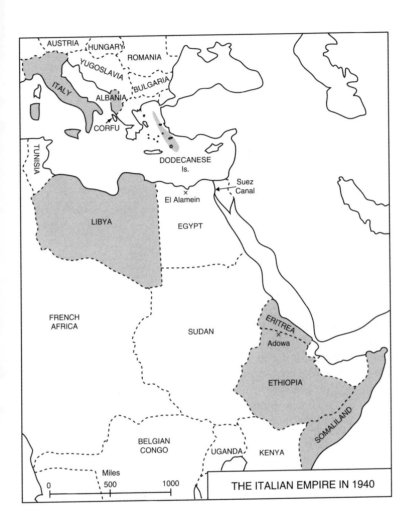

THE ITALIAN EMPIRE IN 1940

Note on usage

The issue of when and when not to promote 'fascism' and 'fascist' to 'Fascism' and 'Fascist' is not one that can be resolved in an unchallengeably 'correct' way. An attempt at indicating some quite important distinctions nevertheless does need to be made. Here, an initial capital is applied to what might reasonably be regarded as an official label: hence the Fascist Party, the Fascist regime or just plain (Italian) Fascism. Capitals have been dispensed with when referring to (for example) European fascist movements, fascism as a 'generic' phenomenon, or the Italian movement and its members before Mussolini's assumption of the Italian premiership.

1
Introduction

The present-day visitor to Rome is surrounded by architectural reminders of past centuries and dead regimes: most notably, those of Republican and Imperial Rome and of the medieval and Renaissance papacy. Here and there may also be observed traces of another bygone regime, one that can seem somehow more distant and elusive than any of these. One of the approaches to Italy's Olympic stadium, for example, is along an avenue decorated with defaced stone columns and crumbling mosaics, obviously inspired yet not produced by classical Rome, commemorating epoch-making military victories, and praising a now-dead leader or *Duce*. The Duce was Benito Mussolini and the regime responsible for thus inscribing his achievements in stone was the Fascist regime he headed. Another face of Fascism awaits the visitor who ventures out to the south-western suburb of EUR, where an array of architecturally innovative, modernistic buildings reminds Romans of a 'Universal Exhibition', planned for 1942 but never actually held.

Mussolini and Fascism dominate the history of Italy between 1922 and 1945. From October 1922 until January 1925 Mussolini, backed by his Fascist Party, was Italy's constitutional prime minister. From 1925 until his dismissal by King Vittorio Emanuele in late July 1943, Mussolini was Italy's dictator and the Fascist Party its state party. Finally, from his initial deposition until his death in late April 1945, Mussolini served as head of Hitler's puppet Fascist state, the Italian Social Republic.

Italian Fascism aroused violent disagreement among its European contemporaries. Its many admirers, most but by no means all of them on the right of the political spectrum, tended to view it as a spontaneous eruption of patriotic energy which, once in power, replaced the fumblings of parliamentary liberalism and the threat of left-wing revolution with order, efficiency and national pride. To its detractors these gains appeared superficial or downright non-existent. For most of those on the left, Fascism was a product of capitalist crisis and its role was to serve the interests of big business and rural landlords. Liberal critics struggled to find a coherent explanation for Fascism, but were viscerally repelled by what they saw as its essential characteristics: hooliganism and thuggery in opposition, and systematic repression in power. In the eyes of liberals and left-wingers alike, Fascism meant the suppression of free speech, discussion and assembly, and the elimination of political parties and trade unions: all this by a corrupt, brutal regime and a megalomaniac leader increasingly obsessed with dreams of imperial conquest. Contemporary debate over Italian Fascism became part of wider debates over what came to be regarded as a general, Europe-wide 'fascism' of which German National Socialism was the most important variant.

Nowadays, although in the English-speaking world discussion of Italian Fascism's origins, character, achievements and responsibilities may be confined largely to academic circles, in Italy itself the Fascist years are still sufficiently recent for academic debate to spill over into the mass media and engage a wider audience. That audience already exists, thanks to Italians' consciousness of and sensitivity to the legacy of Fascism. In the early twenty-first century the Mussolini family retains a high public profile, one of its members as a prominent right-wing politician. A political party, the National Alliance, with a recent neo-Fascist pedigree, occupies posts in the right-of-centre Berlusconi government of 2001–6. And even as this introduction was being written (in winter 2005–6) a well-known Italian footballer won notoriety in some quarters, congratulation in others, for his unapologetic, celebratory use of the straight-armed fascist salute and his open admission of admiration for Fascism.

But what *was* Fascism? How and why did it emerge and win power in Italy? How and with what consequences was that power exercised? These are the principal questions that this short book seeks to explore and, where possible, answer. Fascism, it will become clear, cannot be explained entirely in terms of Mussolini himself, important as his contribution undoubtedly was. Nor can it be dismissed, as in some circles it used to be, as a mere capitalist conspiracy or an irrational outburst of peculiarly 'Latin' violence. A product of the post-war crisis of 1918–22 it may in part have been, yet there is also more to it than this. Fascism, in order to prosper, required a distinctive socio-economic environment, just as in order to challenge for power it needed a political vacuum into which to move and a unique set of circumstances to provide opportunities that otherwise might not have arisen. Having attained power, Fascism faced chronic domestic problems to which it offered its own (sometimes but not always novel) solutions, and pursued foreign policies for which it eventually became notorious. In order to understand these and many other aspects of Italian Fascism we must first examine the setting within which it appeared and from which it was never wholly to escape: the 'liberal' Italy born in 1861.

2
The setting: liberal Italy, 1861–1915

Politics and society in liberal Italy

The modern Italian state came into being during the course of little more than a decade. Between 1859 and 1870 the interaction of nationalist sentiment among limited sections of the population, the influence and involvement of foreign powers, and the ambitions of one Italian state, Piedmont, created a united Italian kingdom. The *Risorgimento* ('resurgence' or 'revival'), as the movement for and achievement of Italian nationhood is commonly known, bequeathed to Italy a complex legacy, of which two threads mainly concern us here: it aroused among politically conscious Italians exaggerated expectations concerning Italy's immediate prospects of power and prosperity; and in forging a new nation without involving or satisfying the mass of the population it threw up a socio-political system riddled with potential weaknesses.

The new state was endowed with a limited monarchy (that of Piedmont elevated to the new national stage), a liberal-parliamentary constitution and political system, and a highly centralized administration. From the start it was widely considered in Italy's other regions to be – and accordingly resented as – an agent of 'Piedmontization'. This was particularly the case in central and southern Italy. Levels of national consciousness were uneven and, throughout much of rural, provincial Italy, extremely low; loyalties to suddenly fallen dynasties and rulers – notably the Bourbons in Naples and Sicily and the papacy in its former central Italian territories – and to the regional traditions they embodied persisted. For millions of peasants the only reality was the locality, any outside authority being regarded as an intruder and potential exploiter. Economic and cultural differences aggravated regionalism and localism: much of southern Italy was barren, impoverished and isolated from progressive developments. The Austrian statesman Metternich had once called Italy a mere 'geographical expression'; now it resembled a mere political expression. As the Piedmontese statesman D'Azeglio remarked, 'We have made Italy – now we must make Italians.'

The gulf between the new Italian state and so many of its people was reflected in, and widened by, the workings of liberal politics. The electoral base of late nineteenth-century liberalism was narrow at its outset and widened only slowly. From around half a million male Italians out of a population of approximately 32 million in 1870, the electorate expanded to some 2 million following the electoral reform of 1881, and stood at 3 million on the eve of a long overdue major electoral reform in 1912. (For the sake of comparison it is worth noting that Spain, another large, Latin, 'Mediterranean' country which, nevertheless, few Italians would have cared to regard as more advanced, introduced universal male suffrage in 1890.) For three decades after 1870 political office in Italy was monopolized by the limited layer of mainly upper-middle-class Italians who had risen to prominence and power during the Risorgimento. Increasingly referred to by the revealing term 'political class', these privileged men, divided not by fundamental differences of belief or class so much as by regional loyalties and personal rivalries, treated Italy to a system of parliamentary politics which lacked clear party boundaries. Instead, through the practice known as *trasformismo* ('transformism'), premiers and their parliamentary managers fashioned constantly shifting majorities by extending favours to deputies and their constituencies. Elections, as much after the 1881 reform as before, were characterized by the bribery, manipulation, intimidation and outright coercion of voters by local power-cliques and political 'bosses'. Parliament in consequence represented the political class itself and those bound to its members by family, local and economic ties in networks nowadays known as 'clienteles'.

Many of these features of Italian parliamentary politics were broadly comparable with those present at the time in other southern European countries such as Spain, Portugal and Greece. Parliamentary unrepresentativeness in Italy, however, was exacerbated by a factor unique to the country: the official non-participation of Catholics. This was the result of the emergent Italian kingdom's absorption of papal territories during the climactic phase of the Risorgimento in 1860–1, and its final occupation of Rome in 1870. The affronted papacy reacted with hostility to what it considered the Italian state's aggression, effectively forbidding Catholics to take any active part, voting included, in Italian politics. In a country around 98 per cent of whose population were baptized Catholics this might seem to have been a death sentence against the entire political system. However, since a great many Italians were actually apathetic or downright hostile towards the Church, while others contrived to combine regular religious observance with disobedience to the papacy's instruction, the reality stopped well short of that. Even so, most of the more devout among Italian Catholics fell dutifully into line. A constitutional gulf was opened up between Church and state. Anticlericalism became entrenched within the ethos of Italian liberalism, and the possible development of a conservative party based on Catholicism was inhibited – with arguably ominous consequences.

The important anomaly of Catholic isolationism apart, later nineteenth-century liberal politics reflected not inaccurately an overwhelmingly rural society distinguished by traditional patterns of agriculture, high illiteracy and low political consciousness. As long as this scene changed only slowly, liberalism was able to function smoothly, if ingloriously. Its test was to come when its gentlemen's-club world was challenged by rapid change and new socio-political forces.

Italy and the wider world, 1861–96

In the rapidly changing world of the mid-nineteenth century it had been easy for Italian patriots and foreign sympathizers to convince themselves that a united Italy would quickly establish itself as a great power. Such expectations were soon dashed. Thoughtful Italians recognized and sometimes resented the important contribution made by other states, especially France and Prussia, to their nation's creation; from this stemmed the acute sensitivity displayed for decades by both politicians and intellectuals concerning Italy's standing as what has been termed 'the least of the great powers'. The country's deficient natural resources, its low agricultural productivity and its consequent economic backwardness compared not only with established powers like Britain and France but also with another new nation, Germany, were enough to ensure that for a generation at least Italy would remain at best a second-rank power. These difficulties were intensified by the sheer demands of nation-building, given Italy's faster than anticipated achievement of a unity that failed to conceal the aforementioned deep regional divisions and uneven levels of *Italianità* ('Italianness'). While it might have been better had Italy's political and cultural leaders settled for second-class status and concentrated on domestic issues, the mood and expectations generated by the Risorgimento and the climate of intensifying international competitiveness after 1870 ensured that they would instead seek the great power status that Germany instantly acquired.

Italian foreign policy during – and beyond – the liberal era was strongly influenced by two notions, sometimes competing and sometimes combining, of territorial expansion: irredentism and imperialism. Many patriotic Italians considered the Risorgimento as incomplete while large numbers of Italian-speakers remained subject to Austrian rule in the regions of Trent and Trieste. The acquisition of these *terre irredente* ('unredeemed lands') was the dream of Italian 'irredentists' down to 1918. Successive liberal governments were none the less prevented from pursuing irredentist claims by a discouraging international climate and by the implications of Italian ambitions farther afield in Africa. The presence of large Italian communities in, for example, Tunis and Alexandria, the activities earlier in the century of Italian traders and missionaries, and a pride in the expansionist histories of Rome, Genoa and Venice, helped to convince men like the Sicilian-born Francesco Crispi, prime minister from 1887 to 1891 and from 1893 to 1896, that in an age of European imperialism Italy too must play an imperial role. The economic case for empire was flimsy. Italy's lack of financial or industrial wealth requiring overseas outlets reduced imperialists to arguing that colonies would generate wealth for Italy's own enrichment, end her supposed geopolitical 'confinement' in the central Mediterranean, and offer millions of Italian emigrants an 'Italian' alternative to South America and the United States. The danger, which they preferred to ignore, was that colonies would be difficult and expensive to conquer, defend, control, administer and develop, and that as a result they would run at a loss.

Although most of Italy's early leaders were sceptical regarding its imperial destiny, by the 1880s the tide was flowing against them. During 1881–2, nevertheless, Italian ambitions in North Africa suffered setbacks when France occupied Tunis and Britain established de facto control over Egypt. Only the seemingly less succulent prospect of

Libya remained to tease the appetites of Italian 'Africanists' for another thirty years.

Italy's loss of face in North Africa had important consequences. First, annoyance at France's Tunisian coup helped to push Italy into the 1882 Triple Alliance with Germany and the old Austrian enemy, in the new (since 1867) form of Austria-Hungary. Second, imperialist eyes now turned towards East Africa. The small territory of Eritrea was annexed in 1885, followed in 1889 by part of Somaliland. The goal of imperialists such as Crispi, however, was the establishment of an Italian 'protectorate' over all or part of the still just about independent empire of Ethiopia. Their dreams were dashed in 1896 when Italian arms suffered a crushing defeat at the hands of Ethiopian forces at Adowa, where 5000 Italians were killed and 2000 taken prisoner. In the eyes of many Italians, it was not the imperial idea that was discredited by the humiliation of Adowa, but the liberal system for failing to make it a reality; for them and for another generation of Italian nationalists the dream of an East African empire lived on. Forty years after Adowa, Fascism was to make it come true.

Liberals and the challenge of change

To be a liberal in late nineteenth-century Italy was not to be a democrat. For most members of Italy's political class, liberalism meant a limited (though not powerless) monarchy, a parliament elected by and for a privileged minority of male Italians, the separation of Church and state, the free movement of property, and a state that actively defended the socio-economic status quo. It did *not* mean universal male (let alone adult, i.e. male and female) suffrage, governments answerable to a mass electorate, or a state that in socio-economic conflicts was either neutral or active on behalf of the weak. And as long as economic, social and cultural change remained slow, Italian liberalism faced little serious pressure to change.

In the 1890s, however, Italy – or at any rate substantial areas of Italy – began to undergo a belated but far-reaching transformation. In agriculture, the backwardness of which had contributed so much to Italy's general economic retardation, the introduction of capitalist methods and modern machinery created in the fertile Po Valley of northern Italy a new breed of wealthy and enterprising *agrari* ('agrarians'), a numerous class of landless rural labourers, and a significant intermediate layer of estate managers and technicians; in other regions such as Tuscany, where landlords customarily divided their estates among tenant farmers and *mezzadri* or 'sharecroppers' (peasants who were contractually obliged to surrender to the landlord a proportion, often half, of their crop or their earnings), many such peasants found their lives and conditions changing very much for the worse. In the north-western region bounded by Milan, Turin and Genoa, the transformation was more profound still. Here, rapid industrialization at last occurred with the development of heavy industry and its offshoots: iron and steel, metallurgy and engineering, shipbuilding, armaments and automobiles, electricity and chemicals. By 1914 there had emerged in the north a powerful class of bankers and industrialists, closely bound to each other and to a protective state. As well as the new, albeit still localized, modern working class produced by industrialization, another 'new' urban class was starting to emerge: increased educational provision in Italy's fast-growing cities and towns was producing a lower middle class eager to fill managerial, bureaucratic and white-collar positions and to keep its distance from the proletariat. The effect of these developments was to alter radically relationships within northern and central Italian society, generating demands and conflicts which in their turn were to contribute massively to the rise of Fascism.

Economic development affected southern Italy much less than the north and centre. The 'southern problem', shirked by early liberal governments, became if anything more intractable as industrialization and agricultural modernization widened the gap between north and south. For the vast, under-employed rural population of the south an escape was offered by emigration to the Americas – chiefly the United States, Argentina, Uruguay and Brazil – or North Africa; by 1914, when Italy's population was 35 million, between 5 and 6 million native Italians were living abroad. Emigration may have been symptomatic of southern problems and may even have relieved them slightly, but it was no cure. Much of the south remained economically and culturally impoverished, socially stagnant and politically inert, its enfranchised minorities little more than ballot-fodder for the election-rigging which kept liberal politicians in office.

In those regions where rapid change did occur, however, novel political developments naturally followed. Electoral reform in 1881 enfranchised mainly middle-class Italians in urban settings where election-rigging was soon to become more difficult than liberal politicians had anticipated. The result was the election of a significant cluster of radical and republican deputies; openly critical of liberal inertia, these groups pressed for further suffrage reform and for government to be more responsible to parliament. In 1892 another form of political opposition, potentially more threatening to Italy's liberal oligarchy, appeared with the foundation of the Italian Socialist Party (PSI). Very soon, despite the limitations of the franchise and being banned during the mid-1890s, the PSI expanded into a significant political force. After the turn of the century socialist (and in some districts anarchist) trade unions attracted increasing support from industrial workers and agricultural labourers, chiefly in northern Italy but also now in parts of southern regions such as Sicily and Apulia. This growth occurred against a background, during the 1890s, of widespread and in places bitter social and labour unrest, to which the authorities, especially during the premierships of Crispi and Di Rudinì, responded – as liberal employers expected them to do – with a policy of repression. Largely in response to the emerging challenge of a materialistic and 'godless' socialism, Italian Catholics from the turn of the century began to abandon their isolation, participating increasingly in politics and setting up their own trade unions. Although at the century's turn a Catholic political party was still almost two decades away, the tectonic plates of Italian politics were starting to move.

From liberalism to democracy?

For parliamentarism and some – obviously changed – form of liberalism to survive, it was vital that Italy's political system and its leading political figures adapt to these changes. While radical liberals showed a willingness to do so, conservatives on the right of the liberal spectrum were unwilling to accept increasing parliamentary assertiveness or to seek to understand the roots of social distress and disturbances. On the contrary: during the 1890s, and particularly between 1898 and 1900, political and military conservatives sought to bring about a return to a more authoritarian system of government. They failed, thanks partly to their own incompetence and loss of nerve but also to the resolute resistance of more genuinely liberal and democratic elements – but the reluctance of conservative so-called liberals to countenance genuine parliamentary democracy remained evident and ominous.

The rallying of what might be termed more authentically liberal and democratic forces to overcome the apparent threat of authoritarianism was nevertheless an encouraging development. The new century, indeed, brought a real, albeit still controversial, attempt to open the liberal system to new currents. Its chief architect was the dominant liberal statesman of the century's first two decades, Giovanni Giolitti. During three pre-First World War terms as prime minister (November

1903–March 1905, May 1906–December 1909 and March 1911–March 1914), and by exercising powerful influence when out of office, Giolitti sought to draw the emergent popular forces of socialism and Catholicism into the parliamentary framework through, respectively, an impartial attitude towards labour disputes and a cooling of traditional liberal anticlericalism. Contemporary critics charged, and many later historians have argued, that Giolitti lacked a true democratizing vision or strategy. At best – the argument runs – he sought, by conceding just enough but no more to new forces, to preserve the essential features of traditional liberalism; at worst, he was concerned mainly to bolster his own position. However much validity there may be in these charges, Giolitti's strategy at least offered some chance of involving more Italians in the nation's affairs, and of steering liberalism through a period of great change. The growing pragmatism of leading Catholics, and the initially strong tendency towards moderation within the Socialist Party leadership, made the strategy feasible amid the economic buoyancy of 1901–7. In 1912 Giolitti's electoral reform tripled the electorate to almost 9 million, suddenly giving Italy near-universal male suffrage.

By this time, however, Giolitti's strategy was collapsing. The economic boom slowed from 1907–8, and in 1911 Giolitti committed Italy to the seizure of Libya from the fast-declining Ottoman Empire. This temporarily appeased conservative liberals, the far-right Nationalists, and assorted imperialists of different political colours, but alienated most socialists and helped strengthen the hand of the PSI's increasingly powerful and vociferous left wing. Among the most militant socialist opponents of the Libyan war was the 28-year-old Benito Mussolini. At the 1912 national congress of the PSI, the revolutionary left succeeded in taking over the party organization. Socialist advances at the 1913 general election, and the wave of strikes and near-revolutionary activity that followed, exposed the limitations of Giolitti's achievement: Italian liberalism had yet to solve the problems presented by the advent of mass politics. The liberals were to have but one more opportunity.

It is nevertheless important to stress that however problematical may have been the condition of Italian liberalism – or what from 1913 can perhaps be termed liberal democracy – as Europe stumbled towards the cataclysm of 1914–18, it cannot be regarded as having been doomed. Without the war and its consequences, all manner of things would have been different and all manner of opportunities for peaceful political change might still have presented themselves. And if the eventual collapse of Italian liberal democracy was as yet far from inevitable, the particular shape of its collapse – the appearance of Fascism and its seizure of power – was as yet unimaginable.

Critics of liberalism

In the later part of the nineteenth century and the early years of the twentieth, most European countries with parliamentary political systems witnessed the appearance of cultural and political groups hostile both to the workings of parliamentary liberalism and to the principles of tolerance and pluralism that underlay them. Italy was no exception. National humiliation in North and East Africa and the rise of socialism at home inspired a vociferous minority of Italian intellectuals to attack liberalism in terms that carried appeal for a growing number of the educated young. The poet Gabriele D'Annunzio, for example, thrilled his readers with his assaults on supposed liberal decadence and his exaltation of violence. His views overlapped, despite marked diffences of tone, with those of the Futurists, a literary, artistic and semi-political movement led by Filippo Marinetti, who extolled physical power, modern technology and war. From a different perspective, the 'elitist' theorists Vilfredo Pareto and Gaetano Mosca gnawed away at the very principles of liberal democracy, asserting that the emergence of ruling elites within all political systems was inevitable, desirable, and deserving of active encouragement – indeed, of formal institutionalization.

This restlessness assumed its most political form and its sharpest focus in Italian Nationalism. Leading figures within the Italian Nationalist Association, founded in 1910, included Enrico Corradini and two future architects of the Fascist state, Luigi Federzoni and Alfredo Rocco. The Nationalists placed the responsibility for Italy's economic backwardness and low international standing squarely at the door of liberalism. They accused their country's liberal political class of weakness and corruption, and castigated liberalism itself, as a system of ideals and institutions, for allowing national unity and strength to be weakened by divisions and conflicts of class, culture and ideology. Symptomatic of this was the growth within the liberal system of the most divisive and threatening force of all: what Corradini termed 'ignoble socialism'. The Nationalists' proposed cure for the alleged ills of liberalism was its replacement by openly authoritarian government, presiding over unrestrained capitalist development and an imperialist foreign policy. Enforced solidarity among all social classes within a 'proletarian nation' like Italy would, they insisted, make possible the maximization of the country's productive energies and enable it, through imperialism, successfully to challenge 'plutocratic' nations like Britain and France.

Although the Italian Nationalist Association attracted significant support among young patriots within the educated urban middle class, its leaders made no attempt to become a real mass movement. As frank elitists they preferred the strategy of what a contemporary English counterpart, Hilaire Belloc, called 'influencing the influencers', establishing important contacts and leverage among conservative politicians, Catholics, and the business community.

While squarely on the political right, the Nationalists came, in the years before the First World War, to occupy common ground with maverick elements of the left. During the first decade of the twentieth century a current known as 'revolutionary syndicalism' broke away from the PSI. Widespread throughout much of Europe before 1914, syndicalism was a strand of militant leftism which rejected political action via parties and parliaments in favour of revolutionary trade unionism. Italian revolutionary syndicalists such as Edmondo Rossoni challenged the PSI with a strategy in which the trade union would be not only an agent of revolution but also the basis of a new social order. By 1914 some syndicalists had moved further. Still wrestling with the application to Italy of the Marxist ideas that had once attached most of them to the PSI, they had nevertheless come to the view not only that the party would never achieve revolution, but that neither, in present or foreseeable circumstances, would the Italian working class. Crucially, they concluded that the source of Italy's ills was not the power of Italian capitalism but its weakness, and that the responsibility for this lay with the political class. The liberal establishment, they therefore decided, must be overturned by a revolution of all 'productive forces' from middle-class entrepreneurs to workers. This position was not identical with that of the more conservative Nationalists, yet the two groups' shared antagonism towards liberalism and PSI socialism drew them together into an embrace which helped to spawn Fascism. Here again, however, it is necessary to stress that as 1914 dawned there was nothing inevitable or even clearly foreseeable about this still unlikely convergence. What truly initiated a process that would take another decade was the advent of a European war and the response of Italians to it.

3

The seedbed of fascism

Italy at war, 1915–18

The outbreak in August 1914 of what was to become the First World War immediately involved five great powers – Britain, France and Russia (the Entente) on one side, and Germany and Austria-Hungary (the Central Powers) on the other. Serbia, whose confrontation with Austria-Hungary had sparked things off, took the Entente side from the outset, while the Ottoman Empire joined the Central Powers at the end of October 1914. Several other European countries took longer – weeks, months or even years – over deciding whether or not to intervene. In some, hot debate erupted among both political elites and the wider public – in Spain, for example, which then remained neutral throughout, and in Portugal, which eventually intervened on the side of the Anglo-French-Russian Entente. In two more southern European countries – Greece, where it literally divided the country in what amounted to civil war, and Italy – the debate was particularly bitter and its effects enduring. Italy stood apart as the only supposedly great power, and the only power entangled in the treaty commitments which had developed in Europe since the 1880s, to undergo such an experience.

The dispute over the rival merits of intervention and neutrality, which lasted from the outbreak of war until late May 1915, inflicted major damage on Italy's political fabric. As far as can be estimated, the majority of politically conscious Italians were to be found in the neutralist camp. Foremost among them were three elements: the overwhelming majority of PSI socialists, hostile to a 'capitalist' and 'imperialist' war; Catholics, strongly influenced by a pro-Austrian papacy and reluctant to fight alongside protestant Britain and anticlerical France against mainly Catholic Austria; and moderate, 'Giolittian' liberals, fearful of the possible effects of war on Italy despite their pro-Entente sympathies. The interventionists were if anything an even more mixed bunch. On what was still considered the left they included revolutionary syndicalists, a few dissident (mainly southern) socialists, and an assortment of radicals, republicans and democrats. For these groups and for others like Marinetti's Futurists, it was vital that Italy commit itself to the forces of progress as represented by the Entente democracies. The more revolutionary interventionists were further attracted by the prospect most feared by the Giolittian liberals: that the domestic effects of Italian involvement might unleash social and political upheaval and thereby give birth to an entirely new political order. On the interventionist right stood the most conservative liberals and of course the Nationalists. The latter put aside their admiration for German authoritarianism in the hope of Italy's acquiring, as the ally of Britain and France, Austrian territory to the north-east and around the Adriatic, as well as Middle-Eastern colonies at the expense of a decaying Ottoman Empire. Intervention on the side of Italy's Triple Alliance partners held few such attractions. Some conservative liberals like Antonio Salandra, prime minister from March 1914, also shared the Nationalists' hopes – starkly contrasting with those of the interventionist left – that participation in what they believed would be a short, victorious war would forge a new solidarity among the increasingly divided people of Italy and facilitate a strengthening of state authority. During the winter of 1914–15 and into the spring of 1915 the debate rose in intensity, spilling over noisily and sometimes violently into the streets of Italian cities. A climax was reached after 26 April 1915 when Italy signed the Treaty of London and committed itself to the Anglo-French cause. Parliamentary approval, while not constitutionally necessary, was still important before war could be embarked upon; for almost a month, until overwhelming parliamentary support for intervention was given on 20 May, the streets of leading Italian cities rang loud with demonstrations orchestrated by Nationalists, Futurists, and syndicalist-inspired squads calling themselves *Fasci di Azione Rivoluzionaria* ('Revolutionary Action Groups': FAR). Although the word *'fascio'*, employed to mean a group formed

15

for political purposes, at this stage possessed left-wing connotations, recalling leftist Sicilian *fasci* active during the 1890s, the FAR represented the first organized foretaste of the fascism of the 1920s. Although in reality the crucial decisions regarding intervention were taken by conservatives such as Prime Minister Salandra and King Vittono Emanuele III, much of the credit was stolen by FAR militants and others who demonstrated during what they came to mythologize as 'Radiant May'. One such, as we shall shortly see, was Benito Mussolini.

The war proved a much longer and vastly more demanding struggle than most conservative interventionists had anticipated, and did nothing to reward their hopes for a new, close and permanent bonding of people, nation and state. On the contrary, and as left-wing interventionists had anticipated, its impact on Italy's society and politics was great and convulsive. Some 5.9 million Italian men were conscripted, of whom over 4 million actually served in the war zone on the mountainous Italian–Austrian border. Italian casualties were high: over half a million killed, 600,000 captured, and a million wounded, of whom 450,000 found themselves permanently disabled. The pain was unevenly spread: Italy's infantrymen were mostly peasant conscripts, many torn for the first time from their native region to serve, for reasons they ill understood, a country with which their sense of identification was imperfect. Few as a result can have felt much enthusiasm for the Italian cause, and as time passed their resentfulness grew. The principal target of their anger was the distant governing class that had sent them to the front with little or no promise of ultimate material reward. Not far behind, however, came the neutralist PSI and the industrial workers, mostly exempt from military service. Grievances also existed higher up the social and military hierarchy. Some 140,000 new officers were created during the war, mostly from among educated young middle-class Italians. Many of these, whatever their initial attitude towards the war, developed at the front a strong sense of comradeship, identification with the war effort and with expansionist war aims, and mistrust of the politicians at home, which were to have important peacetime repercussions.

As well as the impact it had upon active participants, the war also brought profound changes to Italy itself. Most significant was the rapid growth and increased concentration of those industries most closely linked with war production: metallurgy, engineering, shipbuilding, armaments, chemicals and automobiles. Any suggestion of a lasting boom was nevertheless misleading, for Italy's war machine demanded and consumed industrial products of a kind and at a rate no peacetime

16

economy was likely to match. This was all the more serious in view of the accompanying growth and increased unionization of the industrial working class. A distorted economy, potentially short of raw materials and export outlets and unable to benefit from a healthy domestic market, was a sure recipe for post-war difficulties. Returning troops, who would be among the principal sufferers in such a situation, would hardly be mollified by the sight of others who had got rich while they were facing death at the front: not only financial and industrial profiteers but also ambitious peasants who had seized wartime opportunities to buy more land. Meanwhile, the political situation looked more and more discouraging. With the neutralist Giolitti on the sidelines, three wartime premiers – Salandra (March 1914–June 1916), Paolo Boselli (June 1916–October 1917) and Vitttorio Emanuele Orlando (October 1917–June 1919) – struggled unconvincingly to conduct government without him. To many Italians, liberal government was coming to seem ineffectual and irrelevant.

The crisis of Italy's war came in October 1917 with the calamitous Austrian defeat of Italian forces at Caporetto. In a few weeks 10,000 Italian troops died, 300,000 were wounded and 300,000 were captured by the Austrians, whose army drove seventy miles into Italian – and former Austrian – territory. The defeat, though reversed in the dying weeks of the war at Vittono Veneto, shocked Italian public opinion, produced an unprecedented rallying to the war effort, and galvanized the Orlando government into an overdue propaganda campaign. Too late, probably, to do any lasting good, the politicians' commitment to democracy was positively affirmed while Italy's peasant troops were promised land and improved treatment when the war ended. Another event, occurring simultaneously with Caporetto, may well have stimulated the politicians' resolve and certainly was to influence subsequent events: the Bolshevik revolution in Russia.

Post-war crisis and convulsion

Official propaganda following the disaster of Caporetto, aimed at raising spirits and rallying public support for the war effort, made much of the better future that supposedly awaited Italians once victory was won and the fighting was over. Any optimism generated by such messages was quickly dissipated, however, once peace returned and the reality of Italy's post-war condition became apparent. The Italian economy was afflicted by a succession of overlapping crises: food and raw material shortages during 1918–19; acute inflation, beginning during the war and continuing down to 1921; and, as 2.5 million demobilized ex-servicemen returned home from early in 1920, rapidly rising unemployment.

These problems confronted Italy's political system just as it was suddenly readjusting to a world of mass politics to which many of its practices and most of its personnel were ill-attuned. The onset of war had deprived the country's political elite of any chance to adjust gradually, and in what might loosely be termed 'normal' conditions, to the advent of near-universal male suffrage. There now followed another radical change in the rules of the political game, as proportional representation, favouring modern, organized parties over traditional clientelist politics, was introduced for the 1919 elections in fulfilment of wartime democratic promises. The two largest parties to emerge from the electoral reforms and the 1919 polls were the PSI and a new force, the *Partito Popolare Italiano* (Italian Popular Party: PPI). The PSI not only made its mark at parliamentary level but, in local elections, won control of many towns and cities across northern Italy. The PPI, a Catholic party founded in January 1919 by a Sicilian priest, Luigi Sturzo, represented the culmination of Catholic integration into the Italian political system that had begun around the turn of the century. It was established with papal approval, and while officially independent of the Vatican's control, was always to be sensitive to its influence and pressure.

Almost overnight the future of Italy's fledgling democracy – for such it could now properly be called – came to rest largely with these two mass parties, creatures and symptoms of a new kind of politics that the shrinking but still substantial rump of parliamentary liberals found bewilderingly alien. Neither the PSI nor the PPI was remotely strong enough to govern alone, yet despite common ground between moderate socialists and reformist *popolari* (PPI members), the mutual antagonism of the socialist left and the Catholic right blocked any prospect of a reformist coalition which, boosted by groups of republicans and radical liberals, might have guided Italy into a genuinely democratic era. Power, or rather ministerial office and what proved increasingly to be the mere shadow of power, thus reverted by default to the old liberal cliques. Four products of the old regime – Francesco Nitti (June 1919–June 1920), Giolitti (June 1920–July 1921), Ivanoe Bonomi (July 1921–February 1922) and Luigi Facta (from February 1922) – occupied the premiership between the end of the war and the climactic events of October 1922. These three years were to show how limited

18

were the liberal leaders' capacities for coping with a transformed political environment and the forces it now reflected.

Two overriding issues made post-war government difficult: social unrest and nationalist grievance. Strikes and 'illegal' occupations began to affect both industry and agriculture during the last year of the war and reached a peak during the *biennio rosso* ('two red years') of 1919 and 1920. Trade union membership, which had increased sharply during the war, rose even more steeply in the immediate post-war period: that of the socialist CGL (General Confederation of Labour) from 250,000 to over 2 million and that of the Catholic unions from 160,000 to 1.25 million. Militancy throughout northern and central Italy, channelled by both socialists and, in the countryside, left-wing *popotari*, involved factory workers, rural labourers and poor peasants. The bitterest conflicts arose in the industrial north-west and in the agricultural regions of Emilia-Romagna and Tuscany. Many conservative Italians, terrified like their counterparts throughout Europe of a westward spread of Soviet Bolshevism, interpreted the unrest not as the product of accelerated long-term change and immediate post-war hardship, but as the start of an Italian 'Bolshevik' revolution. The pseudo-revolutionary bluster of the PSI left – the 'Maximalists' led by Giacinto Serrati – certainly encouraged such fears. So, in a different way, did the spread in 1919 and 1920 of socialist power and influence across large parts of northern Italy, urban/industrial and rural/agricultural districts alike. Industrial employers and rural landlords were faced with what, if not the early stages of revolution, could certainly be seen and felt as a major and perhaps irreversible shift in the distribution of power from capital to labour. In reality, however, the lack of genuine revolutionary leadership from Serrati and the Maximalists and the complete absence of Soviet instigation made a successful revolution, or even a serious attempt at one, highly unlikely. In 1921 a minority of outright Communists under Amadeo Bordiga and Antonio Gramsci seceded from the PSI, blunting further, and perhaps finally, whatever revolutionary potential the PSI may have possessed – but without creating a Communist Party powerful enough to carry out the task itself. By this time, in any case, militant socialism was already in retreat. The *biennio rosso*'s climax came in August 1920 when metalworkers and automobile workers occupied factories throughout – and in places outside – the Turin-Milan-Genoa 'triangle'. When the occupations collapsed, the tide of worker and peasant militancy began to ebb.

Industrial employers and the well-to-do *agrari* now found themselves presented with the opportunity for counter-attack. In the changed world of post-war Italy they were increasingly unwilling simply to accept the policy of governmental impartiality towards labour disputes which, introduced by Giolitti early in the century, had since become more or less the norm. During 1920 they accordingly began to seek a new way of ordering the three-way relationship of capital, labour and the state. The anti-socialism of the rich was widely shared, moreover, lower down the social scale, by innumerable less well-off Italians who had been alienated by the socialists' monopolizing of employment opportunities in districts under their control and even more, perhaps, by the socialist left's ill-judged, vocal and sometimes physical hostility towards war veterans of all classes.

The emotional commitment of many ex-servicemen – and other nationalistically-inclined Italians – to the wartime struggle and its aims helped to fuel the post-war governments' second set of problems. While it was certainly true that during the Versailles peace discussions in 1919 Orlando and the Italian delegation were treated as less than equals by the leading Allies, Italy's eventual gains were far from negligible. First and foremost, Austria-Hungary was dismembered. The inability of the new Austrian republic to pose a threat (at least unilaterally) was reinforced by the advance of Italy's north-eastern frontier to the Brenner Pass. At the head of the Adriatic, furthermore, Italy annexed the major seaport of Trieste and much of the Istrian peninsula. These territorial gains, while not extensive, largely fulfilled the irredentist goal of completing the Risorgimento by bringing into the Italian kingdom all Italian-speaking districts save those in Switzerland. In the process they also presented Italy with German and Slavic minorities.

What Italy did not receive at Versailles, giving rise to the myth of a 'mutilated victory', were additional territory around the Adriatic and colonial gains in Africa and the Middle East. One Adriatic city, Fiume, became a *cause célèbre* when in September 1919 it was seized from its temporary four-power occupying forces by a band of Italian war veterans, many of them former *Arditi* or commandos, led by the poet-adventurer Gabriele D'Annunzio. The charismatic D'Annunzio and his freebooters held on to Fiume for over a year, setting up a so-called 'regency' in defiance of both international order and an embarrassed Italian government. Whatever liberal politicians may have thought of D'Annunzio, among large swathes of the Italian public he was a hero. While nationalist zealots lauded D'Annunzio's patriotism and courage, non-socialist revolutionaries watched with interest as he published a constitution, the Charter of Carnaro, which seemed to offer a blueprint for the kind of new state many of them now had in mind. This was hardly surprising, since one of their number, Alceste De Ambris, was one of the Charter's main authors. If D'Annunzio's promulgation of a 'producers' state' provided a model which Fascism was later to embrace, so too did the 'style' of D'Annunzio's regime, with its parades, sloganizing, ritual chants and balcony harangues. By the time Giolitti finally expelled D'Annunzio from Fiume in December 1920, the revolutionary poet had become the hero and leader-in-waiting of countless Italians anxious to repair the supposed insult of 'mutilated victory' and to destroy liberalism without succumbing to 'bolshevism'. Another such Italian, overshadowed for the present by D'Annunzio, was Benito Mussolini.

The making of a fascist

Benito Mussolini was born in 1883 near Predappio, a small town in the north-central region of the Romagna. Part of the papal states until Unification, the Romagna nursed a tradition of rebelliousness which was well represented by Mussolini's father, a republican and socialist blacksmith. The young Benito (named after the Mexican revolutionary Benito Juárez) seems to have inherited much of his father's temperament and general political outlook. An undistinguished and disorderly educational history, blotted by several acts of personal violence, nevertheless ended with Mussolini qualifying in 1902 as a schoolteacher. From then until 1910 he led a varied existence. Two periods of unsuccessful schoolteaching were interrupted by two years (1902–4) in Switzerland as a casual labourer and occasional vagrant, and another two years (1904–6) back in Italy on military service. From 1908 onwards he began to find his true *métier*, that of a left-wing journalist, first in Austrian-ruled Trent and then back in the Romagna in the town of Forlì. There, from 1910, as editor of the town's socialist newspaper and secretary of its PSI organization, Mussolini established a personal power base within the PSI from which in 1911–12 he was able to leap to national prominence. As an outspoken opponent of the 'imperialist' Libyan war and of any cooperation between the PSI and the bourgeois Giolitti, he became almost overnight a leading spokesman for the party's militant left wing. One of the chief instigators of the PSI's sharp leftward lurch between 1910 and 1914, Mussolini, as editor from 1912 of the principal socialist daily, *Avanti* of Milan, initially adhered dutifully to his party's official line by opposing Italian intervention in the European war. By October 1914, however, he had moved to a position of 'active neutrality', sympathetic to France and Britain, and late in the year came out in open support of Italian intervention. As a result he was forced to resign his editorship of *Avanti* and was then expelled from the PSI. As editor of a new paper, *Il Popolo d'Italia* (*The Italian People*), funded by fellow interventionists and by the French, he now committed himself wholeheartedly to the interventionist cause, in which his allies were revolutionary syndicalists, Futurists, radical republicans and right-wing Nationalists: the bizarre coalition out of which he was later to forge Fascism.

Why a socialist and internationalist, such as Mussolini still appeared to be shortly before the war began, should so swiftly have become an advocate of patriotic war remains uncertain and much debated. His earlier socialism was perfectly genuine in its way, as advertised by his enthusiastic support for strikers in Forlì; so, as far as it is possible to judge, was his outspoken condemnation of nationalism. His socialism was nevertheless of a highly personal, even idiosyncratic kind, Marxian in theory yet always closer in spirit to revolutionary syndicalism or perhaps to the insurrectionary republicanism of his native region. For all his anti-nationalism, moreover, his horizons remained essentially and even narrowly Italian; his unforced return from Switzerland for military service and his exemplary term as a soldier hint at a layer of patriotism, intuitive and barely conscious rather than in any sense theorized, beneath the outward internationalism. The key to his political career, perhaps, is that it was not so much capitalism or imperialism that he detested as the Italy all around him, and in particular a political culture and ruling caste with which he failed or refused to identify. This liberal political world formed the principal focus of a hatred for which the PSI provided what was to prove a temporary and conditional vehicle. As for any revolutionary vision, it was perhaps revolution itself that excited him rather than the particular kind of post-revolutionary society desired by most fellow socialists. Events at home and abroad during 1913–14 persuaded Mussolini, like the revolutionary syndicalists with whom he was in touch, that the Marxian analysis was inappropriate to Italy. Within Italy, the practical limits of socialist militancy, culminating in the abject insurrectionary failure of 'Red Week' in June 1914, convinced him that neither his party nor the Italian working class was capable of revolution. Elsewhere, the behaviour of workers throughout Europe during 1914 undermined his previous belief in international working-class solidarity and impressed him – just as he had been impressed, against his better judgement, at the time of the Libyan war – with the potency of nationalism as a force for mobilizing popular passions. Influenced by this double revelation, Mussolini gradually embraced the left-wing interventionist view that Italy's participation in the war would generate a revolution of non-Marxian type which would nevertheless overturn the liberal system and bring a new ruling class to power. It was this revolution to which he now dedicated himself.

The immediate prospects facing Mussolini did not, however, look good. Once the intervention crisis was resolved and the war itself began to preoccupy popular attention, his editorship of *Il Popolo d'Italia* was insufficient to keep him in the public eye. All he could do, in more ways than one, was soldier on. Two years of respectable but undramatic war service ended when he was invalided out following an accident. Resuming the editorial chair of *Il Popolo d'Italia*, Mussolini devoted the next two years to developing and propagating a new, and in the long run highly shrewd, strategy of national revolution. By the end of the war *Il Popolo d'Italia* had abandoned its original claim still to be a socialist newspaper and was declaring itself the voice of 'producers and soldiers' against parasitic liberals and unpatriotic socialists. For the present, it was a voice to which few listened. With the war over and the socialists seemingly ascendant, Mussolini the socialist renegade appeared to have missed the revolutionary boat. Instead of helping to lead the PSI towards the conquest of power, the man some would come to regard as the lost Lenin of Italian socialism lay marooned on the margins of Italian political life. He was not, however, to remain there for long.

4

Fascism's conquest of power, 1919–25

Fascism from birth to mass party, 1919–22

On 23 March 1919 the almost forgotten Benito Mussolini presided over the foundation in Milan of a new political movement, the *Fascio di Combattimento* (Combat Group). Those present at this obscure event – estimates of the audience's size range from around 120 to just over 200 – comprised mainly war veterans (notably ex-*Arditi*), Futurists and assorted dissident leftists like Mussolini himself. The movement's name harked back to the interventionist Fasci di Azione Rivoluzionaria of 1915, which Mussolini had vainly hoped to keep together as a vehicle for post-war revolution. The term *fascio*, once the preserve of the left, was by now commoner on the right, for whose authoritarian devotees it connoted the *fasces*, the bound rods borne by the 'lictors' or magistracy of Republican Rome, and the notion of 'strength through unity' they were held to symbolize.

Mussolini nevertheless did not regard the newly born *fascio* as a movement of the political right. With the war not long over and the shape of post-war politics still to emerge, he and the *fascio*'s other leading founders chose to represent it rather as a left-wing challenger for the working-class support of socialism. Its first declared programme was republican, anti-clerical and democratic, calling for decentralization, female suffrage and proportional representation, the confiscation of excess war profits, worker participation in all industrial management and worker control of public services, the nationalization of the arms industry, a minimum wage and an eight-hour day, and the repudiation of imperialism. What soon proved this programme's most striking feature, however, was its meagre popular appeal. In the November 1919 elections the fascists in Milan – their only significant base – polled under 5000 votes out of 275,000 cast and suffered the collateral indignity of witnessing a crushing PSI triumph. By December 1919, with many leftists already abandoning the movement and D'Annunzio totally upstaging Mussolini as the likely leader of 'national syndicalism', fascism faced collapse. Mussolini held on, however, with some support from wealthy Milanese who sensed fascism's anti-socialist potential, and from summer 1920 the movement entered a new and crucial phase in its development.

The most important elements in fascism's revival were its break-out from the mainly urban bases established during its first year and a parallel abandonment of its initial 'alternative socialism' in favour of frank and violent anti-leftism. The years 1920–2 witnessed the growth of an 'agrarian' fascism throughout much of northern and central Italy, most notably the Po Valley and Tuscany where, especially since 1918, socialist unions and Catholic peasant leagues had come to threaten the power of the *agrari* and the position and status of such 'middling' elements as leaseholders, richer peasants, estate managers and the provincial urban professional class. Fascist nuclei in provincial urban centres such as Bologna, Ferrara and Florence inaugurated a policy of *squadrismo*, involving violence by fascist squads (It. *squadre*, sing. *squadra*) against the organizations, installations and militants of socialism and trade unionism. Initially on a small scale, these activities expanded as early success attracted new members to the *fasci*, and as many sympathizers began to provide other forms of support. Over the two years between the summers of 1920 and 1922, fascist punitive expeditions, organized in the movement's urban bases and fanning out across the neighbouring countryside, became commonplace. The headquarters of left-wing parties, socialist unions and Catholic peasant leagues, as well as left-wing newspaper offices and printing shops, were sacked and frequently burnt down; physical violence and humiliation, through the use of clubs, knives and guns, and the forced consumption of the laxative castor oil, were meted out to left-wing and trade union activists. *Squadrismo*, which drew much of its paramilitary vigour from the contribution of *Arditi* and other war veterans, often enjoyed the benevolence of police authorities and the active participation of off-duty policemen. The squads' unashamed and uninhibited use of violence worked wonders. In the space of a couple of years what had previously appeared the impressive organizational structure of socialist and Catholic rural trade unionism was destroyed across much of central and northern Italy. While strikes and union membership dramatically declined, *fasci* proliferated and their membership expanded; by 1922 most provinces outside the south possessed an extensive fascist organization headed by a *ras* (an Ethiopian word for chieftain[s]). The *ras*, men from a variety of backgrounds such as Roberto Farinacci of Cremona, Dino Grandi of Bologna and Italo Balbo of Ferrara, commanded considerable authority within their own districts and operated all but independently of Mussolini. Although still relatively weak in the south, the fascist movement, which little more than two years before had been reduced to under 1000 members, by mid-1922 numbered over 250,000 nationally.

As it expanded, fascism revealed its social physiognomy. Fascist leaders and activists were recruited from among war veterans, especially former junior officers and NCOs; from the educated middle-class youth, professionals and white-collar workers in towns and cities; and in the countryside from the upper and middling layers of rural society – landowners, leaseholders, better-off peasant proprietors and tenant farmers, estate managers and, most important, the adolescent and grown-up sons of all these elements. Although much has been made in recent years of supposed working-class adherence to Italian Fascism, genuinely spontaneous support from the urban workers and poorer peasants whom the original *fasci* had sought to attract was slow to show itself. However, as the left's organizations crumbled many poorer peasants and some workers did join the fascist movement and its newly forming unions: not so much in a spirit of enthusiasm as out of a self-preservative need for work and protection. Increasingly, moral and financial support, if not always actual membership, was coming from rich *agrari* and, to a lesser extent, industrialists eager to see fascism crush or irreversibly weaken trade unionism and socialism.

What these growing numbers of fascists sought from their movement is difficult to state briefly. For some who had fought in the war and others too young to have done so, fascism, and in particular squad membership. offered comradeship and excitement in a dull and ungrateful post-war world. For the more politically conscious it represented a continuation of war in peacetime, with Austrians replaced as Italy's enemies by socialist and liberal 'traitors'. And for yet more, fascism promised the revolutionary overthrow of liberal Italy's tired ruling caste by a new elite, broadly middle-class in composition, steeled in battle against Italy's foreign and internal enemies, and thereby qualified to govern.

The March on Rome

The Italian fascist movement of 1920–2, it cannot be too strongly emphasized, had no close precedents or contemporary parallels, either in Italy or anywhere else in Europe. It is true that many European countries immediately after the First World War witnessed the formation of right-wing, anti-socialist and anti-democratic organizations, often of a paramilitary kind. Most failed to make much impact or, like German National Socialism, took years to achieve anything. Nowhere else in the early 1920s did a movement closely resembling Italian fascism, appearing as if from nowhere, fluid in form and unpredictable in intentions, acquire such numbers and influence so rapidly. This being the case, it is hardly surprising that so many Italians, in responding to fascism, failed to understand fully what it represented or to foresee what, if encouraged, it might become.

As fascism expanded between 1920 and 1922, and as its behaviour, if not always its rhetoric and self-image, became more nakedly reactionary, its appeal to 'respectable' Italian opinion increased. Liberals were not immune: at the May 1921 general election the *fasci di combattimento*, although not actually a political party, accepted Giolitti's invitation to join a 'national' bloc united by its hostility to the PSI. The 35 fascists thereby elected to parliament took their seats on the far right of the chamber of deputies. Fascism's rightward momentum, largely the product of the militantly anti-socialist role that had rescued it from insignificance, was quite simply irresistible – even for the movement's own leader. In summer 1921 Mussolini, still reluctant to sever totally his increasingly tenuous links with the left, attempted to reach a 'Pact of Pacification' with the PSI, only to find himself obstructed – not for the last time – by fascism's provincial bosses. All thoughts of a political truce were quickly abandoned and the undeclared civil war between fascists and socialists went on. In November 1921 any doubts regarding fascism's political direction and power-hunger withered when the *fasci di combattimento* were reconstituted into a political party, the *Partito Nazionale Fascista* (National Fascist Party: PNF). Its programme was an unambiguously right-wing one embracing monarchism, nationalism, free trade and anti-socialism.

Within a year of the PNF's creation Mussolini was prime minister of Italy and Italian Fascism had negotiated the first stage in its conquest of power. Although fascist propagandists quickly concocted what was to prove an enduring myth of a 'revolutionary' March on Rome, Mussolini's path to high office in late October 1922 was in reality eased by elements of Italy's establishment. For the past year, fascists had been seizing control of city and town administrations, most of them previously socialist-run, throughout northern and central Italy. As they did so, the conviction began to form, not only in political circles but also among 'liberal' intellectuals and journalists, within the Vatican and the Catholic hierarchy, and among industrialists and *agrari*, that fascism must be given its political chance at national level. Not only Giolitti but also his conservative rival Salandra, the prime minister appointed in March 1922, Facta, and other leading liberals were now nursing personal ambitions of forming and leading an otherwise conventional government with minority fascist participation. Incapable of collaborating with any but the most moderate socialists or with Sturzo and the *popolari*, and utterly bereft of any new ideas, the bigwigs of Italy's liberal establishment thus succumbed to the attractions of an accommodation with fascism. In adopting this strategy they were confident that fascism, like many a troublesome political faction before it, could be seduced, tamed and 'transformed' by tasting political office and its succulent fruits; in no time at all, they told themselves, this disorderly but, when all was said and done, energetic, patriotic and anti-'bolshevik' force would be reabsorbed into a liberal system that would in turn be revitalized. Views and judgements from outside the narrowly political world were not greatly different. Businessmen and *agrari*, impressed by fascism's highly practical anti-socialism, confined themselves to hoping that fascist involvement in government would decisively toughen official attitudes towards labour and the left; intellectuals and academics, especially but by no means exclusively those of authoritarian and nationalist persuasion, looked to fascism for an injection of new vigour into an exhausted body politic; and the Vatican, especially after the election of Pope Pius XI in February 1922, was led to expect that fascist entry into government might herald an end to the church–state feud and important concessions to the Church.

In envisaging that fascism might merely be employed to remove the left-wing threat and rejuvenate conventional politics, without being allowed to acquire much real power for itself, conservative and liberal Italians can be excused for not possessing the prophetic powers that would have enabled them to foresee the next 23 years of Italian history. Even so, and quite apart from the contrary evidence provided by fascism's impressive numbers and the rough behaviour of its enthusiasts, by the summer of 1922 it was no secret that most of the PNF's leading figures had something much more ambitious in mind than merely allowing their movement to be 'transformed' into yet another domesticated political faction. Acceptance that fascist participation in government was both indispensable and inevitable nevertheless generated false optimism, not to say self-delusion, within the country's establishment, crucially weakening its members' willingness to resist the dangers (which in any case they underestimated) lurking within fascism. The left, of course, recognized those dangers clearly enough, but, after two years of *squadrismo*, with its organization disarticulated, its numbers falling, and its morale in tatters, it was no longer capable of responding effectively. Proof of this came in August 1922, when the PSI in desperation called an anti-fascist general strike. Its abject and counterproductive failure simply encouraged the fascists to step up their pressure on the political system, and in October plans for an insurrectionary March on Rome, the success of which would ensure fascist monopoly or dominance of government, began to be laid.

Given the likelihood that the PNF would enter government with the next cabinet crisis, the decision to attempt a more militant route to power provides evidence of fascism's farther-reaching if still unclear ambitions. Its preparations were highly public, and were accompanied by demands, climaxing at a mass rally in Naples on 24 October, that power be yielded to Mussolini and his party. Even if a complete fascist takeover, whether via violence or merely the threat of it, was inconceivable, talk of one put the country's authorities under pressure to yield more to fascism than, left to themselves, they would have wished.

As all this suggests, bluff was all-important. Fascism was still a far from irresistible force. Despite its popular support – by late summer 1922 fascist membership stood at around 300,000 – and its control of the administration in several northern towns and cities, no more than 30,000 militants, mostly ill-armed, were actually available for action. The march would easily be squashed were the government to resist and the army, as was to be expected despite the pro-fascist sentiments of many officers, to obey a royal command to do likewise. Either physical defeat or craven surrender would probably have burst the fascist bubble. In the event, however, the established powers made it easy for Mussolini. With fascists mobilizing in the provinces the prime minister, Facta, determined on resistance and on 27 October requested the king's signature to a decree of martial law obliging the army to meet the expected march. Having at first agreed, the king on the following morning changed his mind. Vittorio Emanuele's reasons remain less than crystal clear. He may well have been concerned that fascist sympathies within the army officer corps would provoke embarrassing acts of disobedience. Perhaps, and understandably, he was fearful of outright civil war that might put the monarchy's very future at risk. With even better reason he may have been fatalistic regarding the inevitability of fascism's entry into government and, like many more privileged Italians, at least half persuaded of its desirability. Finally, he was certainly aware of the pro-fascist sympathies of his cousin, the Duke of Aosta, and what this might mean for his personal position were he actively – and unsuccessfully – to oppose fascism. Whatever the explanation, Facta was placed in an unsustainable position and promptly resigned. The possibility of a government led by Salandra, or anyone else, with Mussolini in a subordinate position, collapsed when the fascist leader refused to join any government he did not lead. On 29 October 1922 Mussolini, having 'marched' to Rome by overnight train from Milan, was rewarded with the premiership. Only then, as a decidedly ragged and rain-soaked celebration, did the March on Rome actually take place.

The road to dictatorship, 1922–5

Italy now had a Fascist prime minister but not, strictly speaking, a Fascist government and certainly not a Fascist regime. For over two years Mussolini was to preside over coalition governments from which, of the major parties, only the PSI and, later, the *popolari* were excluded. The future in October 1922 was utterly uncertain. No clear consensus existed among leading Fascists and their active supporters as to whether Fascism implied something temporary or permanent, eventual 'normalization' or a genuine revolution. Equally confused, albeit in a different way, were all those influential Italians who were (in widely varying degrees) content enough to have Fascists in the government, and even Mussolini at the head of it, without desiring a lasting change of regime.

For all his willingness to compromise, at least temporarily, with the Italian establishment, Mussolini himself certainly had no wish or intention to relinquish the power he now held. Nor, however, can he be regarded as one of those Fascist maximalists like Farinacci, Rossoni or Balbo who – in their different ways – from the start dreamed of a radical 'Fascist revolution'. Probably, at this early stage, Mussolini envisaged, rather than a complete political revolution, a drastic revision of the existing system to ensure the repeated renewal of his authority. For a time at least this would have satisfied his new conservative supporters, for whom a Fascist-led government may have been a blessing, and the prospect of greater authoritarianism attractive, but for whom the idea of an outright Fascist regime remained disturbing. For many conservatives the ideal was a 'normalization' of politics once the balance of power had tilted decisively against the left, the unions and the lower classes. Until then they would not exercise the power they still possessed to unseat Mussolini. The dream of 'normalization' was shared by more authentically liberal politicians, who refused to make serious moves against Mussolini in the hope that he might stumble and the way be reopened for a return to old ways and leaders. For them, however, times were changing ominously, as their local clienteles, especially in the south, deserted them for Fascism. Ostensibly more threatening to Mussolini, by virtue of their surviving popular support and their ideological conviction, were the *popolari* and the left. In the event, however, the PPI largely disintegrated after first being dropped from the government in 1923 and then abandoned by the pro-Fascist Vatican. For its part the left, already on the defensive before Mussolini's appointment to the premiership, was then further weakened by the continuing attacks of Fascist squads, the haemorraging of trade union membership, and persistent divisions among moderates, radicals and Communists.

The weakness of opposition and the complaisance of most other political forces allowed Fascism to seize the initiative immediately on Mussolini's assumption of office, and to retain it until the summer of 1924. This said, quite what 'Fascism' meant, and might promise for the future, was anything but clear. As it entered the corridors of power, Fascism was a highly fluid coalition, within which five principal but not always sharply defined or distinct strands were discernible. What might be regarded as the most 'typically' Fascist were *ras* like Farinacci and the tens of thousands of *squadristi*, an unruly force most of whom were far from satisfied with merely a share of power. Even if prepared to view the March on Rome and Mussolini's assumption of the premiership as a revolution (which was stretching the term to its limits), these militants now looked towards a 'second revolution' which would sweep away the personnel of liberalism, bringing greater power to themselves and the social layers they represented. Many nevertheless were as yet unclear or even in some cases unconcerned as to the actual purpose of power. The second strand consisted of those who nursed a rather different, and on the whole better thought-out, conception of

'Fascist revolution': what might be termed the Fascist 'left' led by ex-syndicalists like Rossoni and Michele Bianchi, the PNF's first party secretary. The Fascist syndicalists, who had given early fascism much of its radicalism and (unlike many of their comrades), had stuck with the movement despite its lurch to the right in 1920–2. As workers left defenceless through the destruction of their unions by *squadrismo* began to join the Fascist unions set up by the syndicalists, the latter found themselves with a new power base. Their hope now, as in 1919, was for Fascism to supersede the 'old' left and construct a 'national-syndicalist' state capable of stimulating popular energies and enthusiasm. The third element within Fascism at the end of 1922 comprised 'technocrats' such as Giuseppe Bottai and Augusto Turati, who wished Fascism to be an elitist force of intelligent and educated zealots whose task would be to lead and direct the modernization of Italy. Fourth came the Nationalists, whose political association, the ANI, merged with the PNF in 1923 in the hope of guiding it along pro-capitalist, authoritarian and imperialist paths. Still wedded to the notion of 'influencing the influencers', Nationalists like Alfredo Rocco and Luigi Federzoni applied themselves to using their contacts among the nation's elites to draw Fascism in a direction that would strengthen the state and weaken its own *squadrista* and syndicalist radicals. In this the ex-Nationalists were close to the fifth strand: that made up of conservatives, Catholic 'clerico-fascists' and mere opportunists, all of whom in their different ways were driven by a desire for eventual 'normalization' and an attachment to the socio-political status quo.

As far as dealing with his own movement was concerned, Mussolini's most pressing problems were with the *squadristi* and their provincial bosses, the *ras*. This was because, within a party that remained anything but monolithic, it was in their hands rather than his that much of the real day-to-day power and initiative rested. Their demands for a full-scale Fascist takeover embarrassed a still constitutional prime minister anxious to move cautiously in his relations with conservative elites – the Crown, the bureaucracy, the armed forces, the business magnates and the *agrari*. The dilemma facing Mussolini was a delicate one. While eager, for both personal and political reasons, to establish over the *ras* and their disorderly followers a secure control that had eluded him since the day of Fascism's birth, he was conscious of needing this self-same disorderliness as a warning to enemies and false friends of what might happen if they misbehaved. By the end of 1923 he had made his intentions clear in a manner that conveyed two messages. By unifying the *squadristi* into a national Fascist militia, the MSVN, and by creating a Fascist Grand Council to bring the *ras* within a formal framework he hoped to control, Mussolini went some way, though not yet very far, towards creating a more disciplined party. At the same time, the very creation of these bodies signalled his intention that Fascism should play a permanent role in Italian political life.

The fulfilment of this vision nevertheless demanded a stronger political position than Fascism commanded in the early stages of Mussolini's premiership. Despite parliament's prompt concession of emergency powers to Mussolini and the broad amenability of a comfortable parliamentary majority, this situation might easily change and Fascism's meagre parliamentary representation prove a real weakness. Electoral defeat would of course be even worse. Mussolini's determination to remove such nightmares and strengthen Fascism's political position was soon evident with the passage in July 1923 of an electoral reform, the Acerbo Law, designed to give the leading party or alliance at a general election two-thirds of the seats in parliament. In the event the insurance policy of the Acerbo Law proved unnecessary. At the general election held in April 1924 the official, Fascist-led list of candidates polled 66 per cent of the votes and won 374 out of 535 seats. In the south, where Fascism had been weak before October 1922, the movement was now able to use the customary election-rigging machinery in order to ensure a triumph for the official list; in the north, on the other hand, the contest remained sufficiently real for the left, despite its battering over the previous four years and Fascist violence during the campaign, to poll too well for the government's comfort. Even its own strongholds, Fascism's grip was still not total.

The unprecedented – and quite shameless – Fascist violence which had accompanied the election provoked bitter opposition protests when parliament, now with a crushing and exuberant Fascist majority, reopened. Both inside and outside parliament, the Fascists were now bent on making things unpleasant for their critics. One of the most outspoken was Giacomo Matteotti, a moderate socialist, independent of the PSI. In June 1924 Matteotti was kidnapped by a gang of Fascist thugs and stabbed to death, his body remaining undiscovered until August. When the Fascists' guilt was exposed, Mussolini's moral if not actual complicity was inescapable.

The murder of the greatly respected Matteotti gave a much-needed focus to a widespread unease regarding Fascism that had been present since October 1922, but which many members of Italy's political class had been trying to ignore or pretending not to feel. The ensuing 'Matteotti crisis' proved crucial to the development of a Fascist regime.

Amidst a wave of anti-Fascist sentiment, much of the socialist, Catholic and democratic opposition withdrew from parliament in protest: the so-called 'Aventine secession'. Mussolini panicked and would have resigned the premiership had the king required it. The king did no such thing, his inaction exemplifying the unwillingness of conservatives even now to abandon Mussolini. It is not difficult to understand why. The left's performance in the spring election had been sufficiently robust to feed conservative fears of a 'bolshevist' revival were Mussolini to lose office and Fascism to be discarded. Almost as worrying was the possibility that a rejected Fascism might itself resort to a 'second revolution' scarcely less threatening to their interests and comforts than a resurgence of the left. Instead, Vittorio Emanuele and other members of Italy's establishment probably hoped to exploit Mussolini's sudden vulnerability in order to increase their influence over him and reduce the possibility of a full-scale Fascist takeover. Without conservative help the opposition forces were powerless, even when reinforced by the belated recruitment of prominent liberals like Giolitti, who finally committed himself late in 1924. Mussolini thus weathered the storm and retained office, only to find himself faced with near-mutiny in his own party. The *ras*, now officially known as 'consuls', saw the crisis as justifying not concession to opposition but its elimination; not further compromise with the old political world but its replacement by a new order. In December 1924 they collectively demanded that Mussolini, on pain of deposition as leader of Fascism, move decisively towards a dictatorship. On 3 January 1925 Mussolini made it plain to what remained of parliament that this was now his intention.

5

Italy under Fascism

Party, state and Duce

Considering the uncertainties of the previous two years, the speed with which the dictatorship, once launched, was cemented during 1925–6 was remarkable. The process was both punctuated and assisted by four unsuccessful but highly convenient assassination attempts against Mussolini. The total power effectively granted to him by a law of December 1925 was reinforced by a battery of repressive measures. Political opposition and free trade unions were banned; the free press surrendered to a combination of censorship and Fascist takeover; elected local governments were replaced by appointed officials known as *podestà*; and the essentials of a police state were created by extending the government's powers of arrest and detention, increasing the scope of the death penalty, introducing a special court for political 'crimes', and forming a 'secret' police force, the OVRA (Organizzazione Vigilanza Repressione dell' Antifascismo).

With the PNF now the sole actor on the Italian political stage, it might have been expected that these measures would hand it effective political power. The reality was very different, for the true beneficiaries of the changes were, on the one hand, the apparatus of the Italian state, still manned largely by non-fascists, and, on the other, Mussolini himself: the newly designated head of government or Duce. This outcome was no accident, its principal architects being the two most prominent ex-Nationalist Fascists: Federzoni, who served as minister of the Interior until November 1926, and Rocco, who occupied the ministry of Justice from 1925 to 1932. In obstructing a PNF takeover of the state, Rocco and Federzoni acted in conformity with Nationalist belief in a state strengthened rather than revolutionized. Mussolini's support for their course was crucial, since not surprisingly they antagonized influential elements in the Fascist party itself.

The PNF's condition remained fluid. Its most vociferous members were the intransigent *squadristi*, whose most conspicuous representative was Roberto Farinacci. Their conception of Fascism was what might loosely be termed a 'populist' one, deriving from a collective experience of non-stop, activist excitement involving assemblies, rallies and punitive expeditions, and nursing a belief in the quasi-mystical, pseudo-democratic bond between leaders and led. Although the potential tension between this kind of movement and the responsibilities of power was plain enough, these militants now yearned for a Fascist capture of the state and especially of its repressive apparatus. Other Fascists were by now embarrassed or even repelled by the persistent raucousness and violence of a *squadrismo* they considered negative and outdated. This was particularly true of those who possessed some sort of constructive vision of what Fascism might become: the ex-syndicalists around Rossoni whose interest lay in developing Fascist unions, rather than the party, as the basis of a new order; and sophisticated technocrats such as Bottai who, while seeing an important role for the party, wanted it to abandon the spirit of *squadrismo* in order to become an elitist nursery for Italy's future leaders. By 1925, however, all of these Fascists combined were probably outnumbered by those who, since 1920 and especially since October 1922, had been scrambling aboard the Fascist bandwagon out of conservative or blatantly opportunistic motives. For this ever-expanding body of Italians, the party's organization represented little more than a new route to self-advancement — important as this was, and was to remain, in ensuring and retaining their loyalty.

In January 1925 Mussolini took the surprising step of appointing Farinacci, *squadrismo* incarnate, to the post of PNF party secretary. The move proved an astute one, especially since the Duce detested Farinacci personally and held totally different views concerning the desirable relationship of party and state. For even as Farinacci continued to press for a Fascist takeover, his enthusiastic centralization of the party — intended to prepare it for its revolutionary destiny — actually had the effect of undermining the power and autonomy of provincial bosses like himself and neutralizing the *squadrismo* of which he had previously been chief spokesman. By the time he was manoeuvred into resigning in April 1926 he had fulfilled what Mussolini had expected of him and the PNF was well on the way to being domesticated. The PNF's new orderliness and its future role were enshrined officially in the revised Party Statute of October 1926, whereby the Duce became explicitly – and for the first time – head of the party. The Statute also confirmed the Fascist Grand Council's power (however theoretical this was to prove) to formulate policy. Of more practical significance was the Statute's decree that all party posts should henceforward be filled by appointment from above rather than, as had often been the case at provincial and local level, by election or acclamation. By the end of 1926, given Mussolini's parallel assumption of state-based powers, the party's potential for capturing or even more gradually absorbing the Italian state was thus severely curtailed. Only via a complete change of heart on the Duce's part or some other, barely imaginable, change of national circumstances, could this situation alter. Instead, during the late 1920s and the early 1930s the Fascist Party's subservience to the state became increasingly evident. The process, expressly required by Mussolini, was deliberately assisted by repeated purges of party members conducted by Farinacci's successors in the post of party secretary, Augusto Turati (1926–30) and Giovanni Giuriati (1930–1). While the purges were motivated partly by a desire to reverse the uncontrolled growth that had taken place since the March on Rome, the most notable victims were not so much bandwagon-jumpers as 'old guard' intransigents whose temper and views were out of keeping with the regime's emerging style. During the Turati and Giuriati secretaryships, perhaps as many as 170,000 Fascists, mainly of the 'old guard' variety, were expelled from the PNF. Party office now fell more and more into the hands of those who, like Bottai and Turati, desired a highly professionalized party equipped, if not for a swift takeover of the state, then at least for the subtler strategy of creating a new ruling class by which, in the longer term, the state would be transformed.

Subtler this strategy may have been, but it failed to survive the Turati and Giuriati secretaryships. By the mid-1930s the PNF, far from being the active, dedicated, professionalized party of Turati's dreams, had reverted to its earlier pattern of unrestrained growth. Already by the end of 1933 its membership stood at 1,400,000 and by 1939 it had almost doubled again to over 2,600,000. As it grew it irresistibly became what amounted to an over-inflated bureaucracy, largely devoid of a creative political role. The majority of its office-holders were time-serving careerists, bereft of vision or idealism beyond the hyperbolic nationalism and idolizing of the Duce that were the regime's most salient features. Achille Starace, party secretary for most of the decade (1931–9), was a truly representative figure: utterly deferential towards Mussolini and concerned with propaganda and parades rather than political or social initiatives. The Party's condition was reflected in the social flavour of its membership. Whereas in 1921–2 perhaps a third of PNF members were workers and peasants, as early as the late 1920s it had become an organization overwhelmingly of insecure and ambitious public employees, professionals and white-collar workers; in parts of the south public employees made up 75–80 per cent of members. Farinacci had feared that the PNF, if deprived of the vitality of *squadrismo*, would lapse into a cosy middle age; in this at least he was proved correct. The renewed expansion of the 1930s, even if bringing with it a somewhat more representative social mix, could do little to alter a situation that was by this time firmly established. The Fascist Party and its affiliated organizations had many roles to play, as we shall see, but decision-making power was not among them.

Fascist Italy may thus have been a one-party state, but it was not a 'party state' along the lines of Soviet Russia or even, eventually, Nazi Germany. This should not be taken to mean, however, that the PNF's role within the regime was unimportant; far from it. Quite apart from its mundane yet important role of providing job opportunities for the Italian lower middle class, the Party came to perform numerous vital administrative and politically educative tasks which, given more time and greater support from the top, might conceivably have transformed Italy more profoundly than Fascism actually managed to do. Through such bodies as the Fascist Youth and the *Balilla* or children's organization, it attempted to raise Italy's youth in the patriotic and martial spirit of Fascism. Through the elaborate bureaucracy of the *Dopolavoro* ('After-work') organization it supervised and even enlivened the leisure and social activities of the working population, seeking to compensate workers for their falling wages with a variety of fringe benefits and in the process to 'cure' them of socialism. Finally it created, through the mounting of rallies, parades, sports events and other propaganda-filled activities, a distinctive new 'climate' which immediately struck visitors to Italy and penetrated all but the country's remoter rural areas. What remain in doubt, and much debated by historians, are the extent, profundity and durability of this new climate's transformative character.

Whatever the immediate significance and long-term implications of the PNF's role, however, most of the actual power that really mattered in Italy resided elsewhere: in the traditional apparatus of the state – to which, moreover, the police system remained subordinate; in autonomous centres of influence such as private industry and the Church; and of course in the Duce, an essential ingredient of whose role was his ability to deal personally and separately with these interests. Mussolini's preference for state over party and his taste for personal power were manifested by his own tenure of several ministries. From 1926 he occupied the Interior ministry continuously, while between 1926 and 1929 he held no fewer than eight ministries himself. The deliberately constructed cult of the Duce, which reached new heights (or depths) under the party secretaryship of the fawningly absurd Starace, did not therefore mislead: by the 1930s Mussolini's regime was as personal as propaganda suggested. Whether or not it was also, as that same propaganda claimed, 'totalitarian' will be considered later.

The Corporate State in theory and practice

Italian Fascism's chief claim to political creativity lay in the construction between 1925 and 1939 of the Corporate State, a system purporting to be revolutionary yet socially unifying, to guarantee economic progress and social justice by bringing employers, managers and workers together within a legally constituted framework. Fascist corporativism enjoyed sincere commitment among a minority of regime activists and aroused genuine interest and even admiration abroad. In the non-Italian academic world, eminent political scientists, particularly in the United States, published books examining its supposed workings, while its many political admirers and would-be emulators included the British fascist leader Sir Oswald Mosley and Juan Domingo Perón, future dictator of Argentina.

Corporativism was not the invention of Fascism, however. Its pedigree was long and complex, two main strands requiring mention here. One descended from nineteenth-century Catholic ideas concerning modern society. Socially concerned Catholics such as Pope Leo XIII (1878–1903) were deeply disturbed by the growing social conflict of the day and even more by the advance of 'godless' socialism. For social Catholics, society was naturally harmonious, with conflict due largely to a combination of greed among the rich and the manipulation of the poor by unscrupulous agitators. Society's ills and divisions were curable, but only through energetic, imaginative and above all religiously inspired action to curb greed and exploitativeness on one side, ingratitude and militancy on the other. The answer was to bring together employers, managers and workers in each sector of economic activity within 'mixed unions' or 'corporations'. Thus, for example, all agriculturalists, from the largest landowner, through the estate manager, the smallholder, the tenant farmer and the sharecropper, to the poorest farmhand, would belong to one 'corporation', and all factory owners, plant managers and shop-floor workers to another. These bodies, it was argued, would not only replace class conflict with class cooperation but might also replace geographical constituencies and ideological differences as the basis of parliamentary representation. Catholic corporativism was fashionable and influential throughout much of Catholic Europe from the late nineteenth century down to the middle of the twentieth, and in Italy helped foster a climate of acceptance for a Fascist form of corporativism that was actually very different.

The second source from which Fascist corporativism drew inspiration was syndicalism, with its rejection of party politics and its stress on trade unions as agents both of revolution and of future social and political organization. Initially apostles of class war, many of Italy's revolutionary syndicalists turned to corporativism when they abandoned class conflict and workers' revolution in favour of class collaboration and *national* revolution. Collaboration between employers and workers, they concluded, would assist the entire nation by increasing industrial production. Between 1919 and 1920 this conviction, increasingly termed 'productivism', was incorporated into the constitution of D'Annunzio's Fiume republic. The Italian Nationalists borrowed from both Catholic corporativism and syndicalism in formulating their own theories, whereby corporations would be used to enhance capitalist wealth and state authority.

Corporativist ideas were widely held, if often vaguely grasped, among early Fascists. Between 1919 and 1925 their most enthusiastic and articulate advocates were ex-syndicalists like Michele Bianchi and Edmondo Rossoni, head of the Fascist Labour Confederation (CLF) until 1928. Where 'party men' such as Farinacci wished the Fascist *Party* to dominate Italy, Rossoni and the Fascist 'left' sought to achieve popular identification with the Italian state through 'national syndicalism'. This would involve employers and Fascist unions coming together within 'integrated corporations' designed to control labour relations, determine economic policies and channel public opinion. Other leading Fascists, while no less enthusiastic about corporativism, viewed its purpose rather differently. The 'moderate' Bottai, for example, embraced corporativism with typical technocratic zeal, as an entirely rational, practical way to achieve social cohesion, boost production, and altogether modernize Italy through a kind of 'managerial revolution'. To ex-Nationalists like Rocco, however, it meant little more than a means of disciplining labour in the interest of employers – a perception much of the business community was happy to share.

Although the shifting conditions preceding the firm establishment of Mussolini's dictatorship permitted Rossoni and the Fascist 'left' to pursue their goal of 'integral corporativism' with some vigour, actual progress was fitful. On one side, continued competition from the still active free trade unions deprived the CLF of the labour monopoly its leaders craved. On the other side, employers, and especially those organized in the *Confindustria* (Confederation of Industry), showed themselves predictably unwilling to surrender their independence to the kind of corporations desired by Rossoni and his CLF comrades. The Chigi Palace Pact, negotiated and signed between Confindustria and the CLF in December 1923, promised the latter exclusive bargaining rights with employers – an important step along the road to a labour monopoly – in return for backing down over its pursuit of 'integral corporativism'. Although, foreshadowing the future distribution of power within the regime's corporative system, the employers then failed to keep their side of the bargain, the setback for the Fascist unions proved only temporary. After January 1925, membership of the increasingly beleaguered socialist and Catholic unions collapsed and the Fascist unions were promptly revitalized. In October 1925 the newly buoyant CLF accordingly reached a new agreement with *Confindustria*, the Vidoni Palace Pact, whereby the two sides recognized each other as the sole representatives respectively of labour and capital.

While the Vidoni Pact, with its naked recognition of power realities, contained as much promise of conflict as it did of collaboration, Rossoni and the ex-syndicalist Fascists chose to see it as a staging post en route to 'integral corporativism' and the institutionalized partnership between capital and labour. Over the next two years they were to be sorely disappointed. Even as the membership of the CLF swelled, the reality of the regime's attitude towards labour relations became apparent. Rocco's labour relations law of April 1926 and the much-trumpeted Labour Charter of 1927 brought the Fascist unions firmly under state control and installed a labour relations system decidedly favourable to employers. In 1928 the CLF, now almost 3 million strong, was broken up into six parts, depriving Rossoni of his power base and effectively extinguishing Fascist syndicalism as a serious force. The undermining and eventual *sbloccamento* ('break-up') of Rossoni's empire is best viewed as a stage in the consolidation of an increasingly confident, centralized regime, aimed – successfully – at enhancing Mussolini's position by eliminating a possible source of opposition or difficulty. Not only was it carried out ruthlessly, but such was the growing power of the Fascist state that it took effect with minimal opposition. Rossoni, the voice of the Fascist 'left', like Farinacci, the voice of *squadrismo* before him, found himself reduced to political impotence.

Official discouragement and eventual vetoing of Rossoni-style 'integral corporativism' thus had more to do with power politics than with corporativist theory. In fact it went hand-in-hand with official commitment to *some* sort of corporativism, a commitment embodied in the ministry of Corporations set up in July 1926. Over the next thirteen years the Corporate State came unsteadily into being. In 1930, with its sincere and fervent advocate Bottai as minister of Corporations, a potential corporative parliament was introduced in the form of a National Council of Corporations. Four years later what were by this time the long-promised 'mixed corporations' of employers and employees were finally created: twenty-two of them, each ostensibly empowered to determine wages and conditions within a specific area of economic activity (for example textiles, grain production, the merchant marine, etc.). Lastly, in 1939, a full-scale Chamber of Fasces and Corporations was inaugurated in place of the moribund parliament. It had been a long journey, but the Corporate State was now a reality.

Or was it? Even if corporativism did offer a rational alternative to the conflicts within capitalist society, the Italian attempt to implement it, for all the enthusiasm of the syndicalists and the sincere efforts of Bottai and others, was never a serious one. Once the early thrust of Fascist syndicalism had been blunted and any serious prospect of a 'worker-based' version of Fascism destroyed, corporativism, in practice if not in theory, tilted in the employers' favour. From 1928 the workers' side within the corporate structures was manned not by genuine workers or their chosen representatives but by Fascist officials. Although these officials operated mostly in the employers' favour, it is only proper to acknowledge that it was not an entirely one-way street. Within the corporative bureaucracy lurked a minority of genuine idealists and former syndicalists whose effort on behalf of labour registered at least a few victories. Such exceptions nevertheless did little more than prove the general rule within a system that was soft on employers. The latter, moreover, unlike the workers in the CLF, were allowed to retain their own organizations, notably *Confindustsria*. This enabled them to defend their interests effectively not only within the corporations but also by dealing directly with the government and other state agencies. Corporativism in practice, especially during the depression of the 1930s, thus represented a means of disciplining labour in the interests of employers and the state. As this last statement illustrates, the very phrase 'corporate state' is a misnomer, since the Italian state itself was never 'corporate', instead standing apart from and, crucially, above the elephantine edifice of corporativism.

Mussolini's personal responsibility in all this was considerable. Before 1925 he had sometimes flirted with the idea of a Fascism based on the power of labour, and to this end he continued to claim (at least in public) that Italian Fascism worked even-handedly between capital and labour. This was untrue, not only of corporativism but also of Mussolini himself. In reality, whenever confronted with employer resistance, either to labour pressure or, between 1930 and 1934, to the possibility of genuine and potentially far-reaching corporativist advances, he backed down. For the Duce, corporativism was a matter of pragmatism and propaganda, not of principle. On a theoretical level it was something to which most Fascists could subscribe and over which, indeed, they could even be permitted to engage in limited debate. On a propagandistic level it represented an apparent social, economic and political experiment that was useful for bestowing respectability on his regime in the eyes of foreigners. More mundanely, but no less usefully, it constituted an elaborate façade behind which corruption and exploitation could flourish while the Duce pursued the very different goals which, by the 1930s, interested him far more.

Fascist economic policies and their impact

Fascism was not, and never claimed to be, an economic system. From the start, and despite the earlier left-wing, even in some cases Marxist, loyalties of many Fascists, it rejected the notion, held in varying forms and degrees by most on the left, that the 'ownership of the means of production' – that is, financial and economic power – constituted the fundamental or at least the principal determinant of human relations and politics. Throughout the life of the Fascist regime, it is true, a minority in the Party and the corporate structure continued to feed the guttering flame of Fascist 'leftism' with somewhat qualified anti-capitalist rhetoric. Such restlessness, and the implicit challenge to private wealth it contained, had its uses for Mussolini in his dealings with the captains of industry, agriculture and finance – just as long as he could be seen to possess the power equally to suppress, control or release it. This Mussolini was eminently successful in doing. From his crucial initial compromise with big business and the *agrari* in 1920–2 down to his fall in July 1943, Fascist 'leftism' was never allowed significantly to influence major policy decisions or initiatives.

For all his own former socialism, Mussolini himself knew little of economics and possessed only generalized economic ideas. By 1922 his views on economics, like those of many Fascists, amounted to little more than a commitment to 'productivism': the maximization of industrial and agricultural production in the national interest. Precisely what this meant – how it would be achieved and to what concrete ends it would be directed – was as yet unclear. What can be said, at least with the benefit of hindsight, is that productivism, especially when combined with the 'statism' pursued by the ex-Nationalists and happily embraced by the Duce, did contain significant implications for the long-term relationship between Italian capital and the Italian Fascist state. To put it in a nutshell: Fascism would never *threaten* capitalism but, as the price of survival and, for its individual exponents, continued personal enrichment, capitalism would have to accept a growing measure of state intrusion.

This reality, while perhaps inevitable given the strength of Fascist authoritarianism, was nevertheless slow to take shape. To begin with, Fascism simply had to fit in with a financial and economic framework inherited from liberalism. The ground rules of what passed for Fascist economic policies were therefore laid by such dominant characteristics of the Italian economy, clearly visible even before the war, as the close bonds between state and heavy industry, the selective favouring by governments of some interests at the expense of others, and a weak consumer sector caused by the state's attempts to divert personal incomes, through taxation, into industrial investment. Significantly, there was little here with which Mussolini and other leading Fascists felt uncomfortable.

Even to talk of 'Fascist' economic policies before the start of the dictatorship in 1925 would be misleading. While Mussolini to-ed and fro-ed his way towards greater political power, he and his laissez-faire finance minister, De Stefani, satisfied themselves with simply allowing Italy to share in Europe's post-war boom. Only during 1925–6, with the dictatorship in the process of creation, did serious inflation, balance of payments difficulties and a depreciating lira (Italy's unit of currency until its adoption of the euro) force De Stefani's replacement by Giuseppe Volpi, an industrialist and banker. Volpi's deflationary and protectionist policies set the tone for the rest of the Fascist era, as did the personal intervention of an increasingly confident Mussolini. In 1927, at the Duce's instigation, the lira was fixed at the artificially high level of 90 to the pound sterling. 'Quota 90' had less to do with financial or economic necessity, as conventionally understood, than with Mussolini's conflation of national *interest* with his own perception of national *pride*. The latter demanded 'Quota 90', which instantly became a feature of Fascist sloganizing and propaganda. High tariff barriers were now erected to protect Italian heavy industry and selected agricultural products. From the late 1920s down through the 1930s, Italy's industrial and agricultural exporting sector was largely sacrificed in favour of a sluggish domestic economy stabilized by cartels, price-fixing and, increasingly, state intervention. This last development took place both directly, through the actions of government ministries and agencies, and more insidiously, via the channels provided by the corporate system. General deflation, wage-cutting and the suppression of free trade unions not only implied Fascism's rejection of a vigorous domestic market but also provided a strong indication of its social priorities. These were dominated by a preference for stability over mobility. New and continuous mobility, both vertically up and down the social scale and horizontally from countryside to urban centres, was actively discouraged. None of this meant that these social shifts ceased, which they emphatically did not.

While plainly damaging to some sectors of the economy, Fascist policies unquestionably benefited other, powerful interests whose ability to influence government long predated Fascism and on whose continued acquiescence the regime's chances of permanence partly depended: heavy industry, the *agrari* of the Po Valley, and the less enterprising big landowners of other regions. These agrarian interests were, for example, the principal beneficiaries of Mussolini's much-trumpeted 'battle for grain'. This characteristic combination of policy and propaganda campaign was launched as early as 1925 in the same ultra-patriotic spirit as 'Quota 90', its goal being to free Italy from the cost of importing grain by turning more land over to wheat. In its own terms the campaign achieved considerable success – but only by reducing the range of Italian agricultural production and, therefore, restricting the diet of less well-off Italians. With farmers abandoning olive groves, fruit orchards, vegetable gardens, vineyards and pasture in favour of grain, 'Let them eat carbohydrates', if not one of Fascism's slogans, might just as well have been.

The Wall Street Crash of 1929 and the subsequent onset of the world depression had the effect of nudging the Fascist regime along paths which, it is probably fair to say, many of its leaders in any case found perfectly congenial. The weakness of Italy's banks and their vulnerability to possible collapse led the government to intervene more frequently, and more directly, in the economy. A vital stage in this process came in 1933 with the creation of the Institute for Industrial Reconstruction (IRI), a state holding company for private funds which, in the course of the rest of the decade, increasingly took over from private banks the task of investing in industrial development and activity; naturally, it did so along lines consistent with general government policy. The Ethiopian war of 1935–6 (see pp 61–4) gave renewed impetus to a concept that had always been implicit in productivism, the 'battle for grain', etc., and in 1936 became Mussolini's declared policy: namely, 'autarky' or economic self-sufficiency. The Fascist goal of autarky, total in theory but failing that as close to total as possible, had its roots in pre-1915 nationalism and imperialism. For Mussolini, autarky was essential for a warrior nation that simply could not afford economic dependence on others. The proposition was conveniently reversible. Since within its existing borders Italy – unlike, it was argued, Britain with its vast empire – had no chance of achieving autarky, it followed that those borders must be extended to obtain what Italy required: vital raw materials, land for settling its 'surplus' population and captive markets for home-produced goods. It further followed, given the unlikelihood of such gains falling peacefully into Italy's lap, that territorial expansion would necessitate military conquest. The fact remained that it would all take time.

From 1935 onwards the Fascist state's role in industrial financing, raw material allocation, the replacement of imported by home-produced materials, and direct control of major industries increased. By 1939 it effectively controlled over four-fifths of Italy's shipping and shipbuilding, three-quarters of its pig-iron production and almost half that of steel. This level of state intervention greatly surpassed that in pre-war Nazi Germany, giving Italy a peacetime public sector second only to that of Stalin's Soviet Union. The difference between Fascist Italy and the USSR lay, of course, in the survival in Italy of a private sector that remained substantial even if restricted in its freedom and increasingly concentrated: for example, two firms, Montecatini and SNIA Viscosa, monopolized the entire chemical industry. The individuals who comprised Italy's financial, industrial and agrarian oligarchy may have mistrusted and even resented the state's growing role, not to mention the dangerous purposes towards which Italy's still uneven economic resources were by the late 1930s being directed. They were nevertheless too compromised, too fearful of a 'bolshevist' bogey the regime worked hard to nourish, and perhaps, at bottom, too *comfortable* to wish to disembarrass themselves of a still largely rewarding commitment.

Disputes continue to rage among historians as to the effects of Fascist economic policies, and in particular their relationship with the 'modernization' of Italy. The issue of 'modernization' will be explored further later; what bare statistics (even if they could be believed) on growth and productivity conceal, however, is the sometimes deliberate and sometimes accidental unevenness with which Fascist economic policies, and the social priorities informing them, affected different areas of Italian society. The most obvious beneficiaries have already emerged: cosseted northern industrialists, rural landlords and agrarian capitalists, their products protected and their wage bills held down by Fascist labour policies. Between the curbing of inflation in 1925–6 and its return in the late 1930s, substantial elements of the urban upper and lower middle class also had cause for satisfaction. Even during the depression of the 1930s, expanding state and party bureaucracies provided opportunities for employment and improved status; an expanding education system created new posts for would-be teachers and qualifications for a rapidly increasing number of middle-class students. In addition, moreover, these middling layers of urban Italian society gained a new sense of security and status from the disciplining of organized labour. The mood of urban middle-class confidence even extended to women. Despite Fascism's ideologically traditionalist and culturally chauvinist view of female roles, economic and social changes proved more powerful than official prejudice. Because expanding educational, medical and clerical services created jobs and positions that women – for subtler discriminatory reasons – were considered best suited to fill, Fascism witnessed an unintended and paradoxical rise in female professional and white-collar employment.

The rural counterparts of the urban middle classes, those small agricultural proprietors, tenant farmers and sharecroppers, many of whom had looked to Fascism for betterment, were much less fortunate. Under Fascism the numbers of peasant proprietors, which had been increasing since the war, declined again, while rising numbers of tenants and sharecroppers found their terms and conditions deteriorating. Fascist propaganda, with its stress on social stability, idealized rural life to the extent of advocated 'ruralization' – a return to the land rather than continued urban growth. Propaganda was nevertheless at odds with the realities of rural existence under Fascism, which, far from reversing the chronic flight from the land, caused it to accelerate. This process, and the similarly discouraged tide of emigrants from south to north, was intensified by the still widening gap between northern Italy, which under Fascism continued to develop and enjoyed relative prosperity, and the south, devastated by policies such as the 'battle for grain' and now deprived of its traditional emigration outlets in the United States and South America. Some headed south to Italy's new 'fourth shore', Libya, though nowhere near enough to satisfy Fascist colonialists or vindicate official propaganda. Even fewer, when the opportunity presented itself after 1936, chose to settle in Italy's new empire in Ethiopia.

The effects of Fascist policies on the working class were mixed, recent historical research suggesting that they were less harsh, in purely material terms at least, than used to be believed. On the one hand, working-class Italians were no longer defended by their own trade unions, were forbidden to organize in their own interests and, as we have seen, derived only limited and uneven benefit from the machinery of the corporate state. Industrial workers suffered officially imposed wage cuts, only partially mitigated by more general deflation, in 1927, 1930 and 1934, while agricultural labourers' money wages declined during the early 1930s by between 20 and 40 per cent. Nor, it is important to stress, did a regime much admired abroad for its 'efficiency' render Italy as immune from the 1930s depression as its propaganda strove – with considerable success – to suggest. Official figures admitted to the existence of a million unemployed by 1933; the true figure was certainly much higher, with millions more (especially in agriculture) *under*-employed, and working-class women forced back into the home. In contrast to the aforementioned growth in middle-class female employment, this last 'development' certainly suited most Fascists (and quite possibly much of the male labour force). The fact remains that once the depression was over this trend began to reverse itself.

Although money wages in Italy may have declined dramatically, it is only proper to recognize, first, that real wages, thanks to falling prices during the early and mid-1930s, held up better, falling between 1925 and 1938 by an average of at most 10 per cent (a figure that some historians would consider too high); second, that the level of unemployment would have been higher had it not been for the regime's investment and public works policies; third, that while the corporate state proper may have done relatively little for workers, the Fascist unions, or syndicates, not only continued to function alongside the corporations but also managed to provide their members (whose numbers increased considerably during the 1930s) with some protection and benefits; fourth, that the Fascist state increased the provision of social insurance (against unemployment, injury, etc.) available to workers; and finally, that new institutions like the *Dopolavoro* undoubtedly did something to cushion the effects of hardship and slightly to enrich otherwise monotonous working-class lives.

Reaching an assessment of Fascism's economic performance is bound to be problematical. The regime was highly skilled at headlining successes and concealing failures, especially during the depression when the shortcomings of more open governments were brutally exposed. Claims for the regime's triumphant weathering of the depression, as well as often depending on false comparisons with far more industrialized economies, can be regarded as testifying to Fascism's success in presentation as much as in hard achievement. Overall, the Fascist regime shared in the European boom of the mid-1920s and the general recovery of the late 1930s, arguably failing to make the best use of either. In developmental terms, and even allowing for the impact of the depression, its twenty-year record was inferior to those of the liberalism that preceded it and the democracy that followed. We cannot know how a liberal-democratic Italy would have performed over the two decades in which Fascism ruled the country, but there is no reason to suppose it would not have done better: probably at less personal cost to individual Italians and certainly with fewer vainglorious claims to be doing something special. Yet in the end much of this may not matter as much as it seems to do. This is because Mussolini, certainly by the 1930s, was simply not drawn to the goals of what might be termed conventional economic policy: increasing Italian exports, stimulating the domestic market, defeating unemployment, raising living standards, or even improving the diet of poor Italians. Ever more a martyr to his own digestive system, the Duce deluded himself that leaner Italian males would also be fitter and more aggressive. This fantasy was of a piece with his conviction, rationalized via the case for autarky, that the ultimate purpose of economic policy was to help prepare the country for its ultimate test: war.

Fascist totalitarianism: myths and realities

The word 'totalitarian' and the concept of 'totalitarianism' were invented by Italian Fascism and remain among its more enduring legacies. Nowadays, thanks chiefly to its association with Nazism and Communism, 'totalitarianism' carries mainly negative connotations. For Italian Fascists, who it must be recognized coined and disseminated it well before the evil excesses of Hitler and Stalin could be predicted, the term and the ideas it conveyed were wholly positive. According to official propaganda and the Fascist theory painstakingly constructed over the years by Party luminaries like minister of Education Emilio Gentile, Fascism was a 'totalitarian' system requiring not just the passive conformity of all Italians but their sincere commitment to, and active participation in, a heroic enterprise of national regeneration. Totalitarianism was viewed as both a concrete goal that would take time to achieve and a 'myth' that in the meantime would inspire Italians onward. For the more visionary Fascists, 'total' dedication to Fascism and its aims would eventually produce not only a new Italy with a new kind of regime, but a new civilization and a new kind of humanity.

Most Italians – and of course most foreigners – paid little heed to the more extravagant maunderings of Fascist theory, much of which was turgid and intellectually mediocre. Many observers of Italian life during the 1930s, especially undemanding foreign ones, none the less concluded from what they saw and heard that the goal of a totalitarian order was well on the way to being realized. It is not difficult to understand why. Whatever Fascism's failures, when it came to presentation it was an extraordinary success. Propaganda, employing sophisticated modern techniques to brilliant effect and cleverly combining traditionalist with ultra-modernist imagery, was all-pervasive. Its dominance went unchallenged owing to the effectiveness with which alternative views were censored and opposition suppressed. The cult of the Duce with its liturgical slogans – 'Mussolini is always right', 'Believe, Obey, Fight!' – was inescapable, managing like other personality cults to transcend an essential absurdity that insulted the intelligence of those who devoured it (and those who still do). Fascist uniforms, officials and militia were everywhere. Trains – at least on the main lines used by people who mattered – ran on time. Malarial marshes were drained and cultivated – chiefly near Rome where the results could be proudly shown to visiting foreigners. Genuinely innovative architecture like that of EUR spoke of Fascism's claim to be 'the movement of the twentieth century', while the exposure of Roman remains linked it with a glorious past. Even the country's sportsmen obliged with success: in addition to the triumphs of its track and field athletes and its cyclists, Italy's footballers won two World Cups (1934 and 1938) and an Olympic gold medal (in 1936) under the aegis of a Fascist regime that extolled physical fitness and prowess.

Italy under Fascism certainly looked, sounded and somehow 'felt' *different* – different, that is, from the country it had been in pre-Fascist times and different from most other countries in the Europe of the 1920s and 1930s. Only other countries ruled by what Sir Oswald Mosley admiringly called 'new movements' – the Soviet Union and the Third Reich – seemed to exude a similar energy and confidence. For those Fascists – and they certainly existed – who possessed a driving, radical vision of a new Italy, a new civilization and a 'new Fascist man', the changes just referred to were more than a veneer; rather they represented the early stages of an ultimately profound cultural and 'anthropological' transformation. For party maximalists, Fascism, with its stress on faith and insistence on obedience, was to all intents and purposes a new religion. For an admittedly untypical minority within this minority, it possessed a world role that had nothing to do with crude conquest. Fascists like Ugo Spirito dreamed that Italy would be the birthplace of a new Europe and of a Fascism whose applicability would be 'universal'. The one attempt at a 'fascist international', held in Montreux, Switzerland, in 1934, confirmed in its squabbling and backbiting what to others seemed obvious: that 'fascist internationalism' and 'universalism' were terminologically contradictory.

How Italy might have looked had Fascism been blessed with more time and a leader more in tune with radical totalitarian ideas we can never know. Nor, for reasons that should become clear in the next two chapters, would we be wise to expend much effort in counterfactual speculation. The Fascist regime must ultimately be understood and judged in terms not of what some Fascists vainly dreamed it might become, but of what most Fascists pragmatically settled for and what it actually was. In truth Fascism fell well short of the totalitarianism claimed – whether as an accomplished reality or merely as a dynamic process – by its disciples, by some contemporary and later political scientists, and even by a number of present-day historians. It is also important to emphasize that the unevenness of Italian Fascism's drive towards totalitarianism and the incompleteness of its accomplishments were due not to extraneous or circumstantial factors but to an *intrinsic* feature of the regime as it developed from 1922 onwards. This was, quite simply, early Fascism's need to make compromises with powerful established interests in order to have any chance of obtaining access to power itself. That need, it may be suggested, was due in turn to Fascism's varied, shifting and confused character and its related lack of an ideology and programme coherent enough to sustain a truly profound revolution. Nor was this a matter of mere short-term, disposable tactics. Throughout the years of his regime's emergence and consolidation, that is from 1922 to 1929, Mussolini maintained his strategy of compromise with Italy's wielders of financial, economic and, later, religious power. The economic and syndical policies pursued after 1925, for example, were in part adopted to placate uneasy industrialists and landowners. It was in 1929, however, following careful preparation, that Mussolini achieved his greatest political stroke thus far. The Lateran Accords between the Kingdom of Italy and the papacy brought to an end their sixty-year-old feud, created the Vatican state, and erected a complete framework for Italy's Church–state relations. For Mussolini the agreement, as well as constituting a massive diplomatic triumph in itself, sealed his alliance with conservative forces and ensured the support – even if often passive – of countless Italian Catholics who might otherwise have been half-hearted or hostile towards him.

The existence of autonomous, conservative interests – monarchy, industry, *agrari*, armed forces and Church – was thus integral to Mussolini's regime as it entered the 1930s. Their continued influence made the regime, in its essential character, less profoundly 'fascist' and less totalitarian in scope than it claimed to be and than outward appearances suggested. Just as Mussolini, admittedly to his perpetual and intensifying frustration, remained until 1943 constitutionally subordinate to the king, so despite all efforts to the contrary on the part of militant Fascists – and, occasionally, of Mussolini himself – his other conservative allies retained considerable autonomy within their respective spheres of operation. To cite merely the most serious example: the Church, notwithstanding sometimes bitter disputes with the government, maintained a powerful hold over two areas of Italian life crucial to a would-be totalitarian regime that made quasi-religious claims on individual loyalties: education and the private consciences of believers. The effect of this diluting of the regime's supposed totalitarianism, ironically, was to enhance Mussolini's personal authority. In return for preserving some autonomy, his conservative allies effectively abandoned any idea of concerted action and surrendered to the Duce an awesome freedom to formulate and implement general, and especially foreign, policy.

Even among the population at large, Fascism's impact was uneven, especially for a regime supposedly set on altering the nation's whole mentality. Throughout much of rural (and especially southern) Italy another of Fascism's compromises allowed existing power structures to survive, either alongside or actually disguised as those of the Party. The village of Gagliano in the southern region of Lucania, immortalized in Carlo Levi's classic memoir, *Christ Stopped at Eboli*, exemplifies Fascism's failure to impinge on everyday rural life, save as the latest in a long line of devices for perpetuating the control of the local oligarchy. Urban Italians might be exposed to Fascist propaganda through school, press, radio, cinema and the various organizations of the Party, but such things barely penetrated the southern countryside. With one southern power group, however, the Fascist regime refused to compromise. In Sicily the Mafia, whose ability to operate its own system of administration and 'justice' was plainly incompatible with 'totalitarianism', was resolutely pursued and apparently suppressed. Yet here, too, appearances were deceptive. As we shall see, the Mafia, an essentially conservative institution with local roots Fascism could neither equal nor destroy, proved capable of surviving underground and of having the last word in its private war with Fascism.

While the hyperactive atmosphere of urban Italy may have suggested otherwise, Mussolini was in reality, and perhaps not too reluctantly, obliged to settle for obedience and conformity rather than the universal activism supposedly central to totalitarianism. On this restricted level, at least, the Fascist regime during the early and mid-1930s recorded considerable success. The coercive capacities of police, OVRA and Fascist militia played a major part in this, as did the enervating effects on potentially troublesome elements of occupational insecurity and the destruction of old political and trade union networks. Fear of dismissal ensured the quiescence of the rising numbers of public employees, most notably the great mass of schoolteachers and university professors who swore an oath of loyalty to the regime in the 1930s. Only 11 out of 1250 professors refused the oath – an apparently shameful piece of cowardice that actually betokened Italian academe's shoulder-shrugging acceptance of a regime that offered little intellectual challenge to established academic orthodoxies. Among Italian youth and young adults, propaganda, the 'fascistization' of education and the conditioning effects of youth organizations, the *Dopolavoro*, etc., if not creating as many passionate Fascists as was intended, did help secure acquiescence. If official organizations and activities failed to win popularity for a party widely and rightly considered corrupt, they did, at least for a few years, make a popular hero of Mussolini. And it is essential to recognize that for many Italians the regime's achievements seemed very real; social peace at home and respect abroad were agreeable novelties to politically conscious Italians previously accustomed to social uncertainty and international humiliation. Fascism's appeal – and it was not to prove permanent – as a regime of order was assisted by the fact that, for all the high-sounding talk, its ideological demands on individuals involved little more than ultra-patriotism and veneration for the Duce. What appears to have been a widespread passive acceptance of the regime during the early 1930s inspired a leading Italian historian of Fascism, Renzo De Felice, to call these the 'years of consensus'. The notion understandably offends both Italians and non-Italians for whom outward consensus cannot be disentangled from the censorship, deliberately misleading propaganda and downright repression used to enforce it. The criticism is a reasonable one, since consensus – if it is to mean anything – implies an active freedom of choice which not even De Felice can convince us was enjoyed by Italians under Fascism.

For two categories of Italians, passive consensus, however achieved, was anathema. The opposition to Fascism, composed from the late 1920s of isolated individuals, small clandestine groups and trade union cells, was courageous but weak, barely succeeding in keeping alive a flicker of resistance which would later grow into something much greater. Many of its leading figures were driven into foreign exile, foremost among them the Roselli brothers of the *Giustizia e Libertà* ('Justice and Liberty') organization. Others, like Carlo Levi, were punished by internal exile to remote parts of their own country. Treatment of active opposition was ruthless, but before the Second World War stopped well short of the excesses that were commonplace in Stalinist Russia and Nazi Germany. Neither pre-war concentration camps nor the casual use of the death penalty for political purposes were among Fascism's repressive devices.

At the other extreme stood those Fascists for whom the regime's accomplishments were insufficient. Resentful of the continued power of the Crown, capitalists and Church, acutely aware of Fascism's failure to bridge the gulf between state and people, and envious from 1933 onwards of the more extreme course being pursued by Nazism in Germany, radical Fascists insistently demanded further advances towards true totalitarianism. Malcontents on what remained of the old party 'left' looked for greater progress in a socially radical, neo-syndicalist direction, but remained just as disappointed. Nothing more graphically illustrates Fascism's limitations as a totalitarian regime than the endless yearnings of its own militants for a 'Fascist revolution' that never came. Only from 1936 did signs of change start to appear.

6

Diplomacy and imperialism, 1922–36

Fascism and foreign affairs

Historians still disagree over Mussolini's conduct of foreign affairs in the years between his assumption of the premiership and the conquest of Ethiopia in 1935–6. Some still hold the view, once dominant on the left, that the militaristic imperialism of the 1930s represented the largely unpremeditated response to domestic problems of a dictator whose chief concern was always the internal consolidation of his regime. More recently, the balance of historiographical opinion has tended to tilt towards a belief in the underlying consistency of Mussolini's foreign policy, the intent of which was always expansionist even when it was conducted in a moderate manner. What has seldom been doubted is Mussolini's controlling hand in the making of policy. Like many a political leader before and since, once in power he quickly developed a taste for the international stage, to which he brought an innate but still blooming certainty of his own genius. As far as the diplomatic sphere was concerned, this translated into an unbounded self-confidence regarding his knowledge and understanding of international affairs and his skills as a negotiator. Never good at delegating to ministers, the Duce, in this as in many other areas, struggled to find a senior Fascist who seemed to him anywhere near qualified to be foreign secretary; for long periods he preferred to do the job himself, and even when not doing so – between 1929 and 1932 when Dino Grandi was foreign secretary and after 1936 when the post was held by his own son-in-law Galeazzo Ciano – there was little doubt where the ultimate power and initiative lay. Although at first his conduct of foreign affairs may have been guided and even restrained by cautious foreign office officials and their permanent head, Contarini, such restraints were soon cast aside, first as Mussolini simply overrode or bypassed his bureaucrats and then as the foreign office was partially 'fascistized' through the appointment and promotion of loyal party members.

Most countries' foreign policies operate along fairly well-worn paths from which sudden deviation is difficult to imagine and even harder to accomplish. Italy in the aftermath of the First World War was no exception. For a combination of geographical and historical reasons, the chief areas of Italian interest remained the Mediterranean, north and east Africa, the Balkans and, more tenuously, the Middle East. The principal determinant of its international position in the post-war world continued to be its economic and military weakness. The latter being to some degree relative to the strength of others, the post-war panorama did offer Italy significant reassurance along its most vulnerable border, where what had been since 1861 a chronic and serious threat to national security was swept away by the dismemberment of Austria-Hungary, the historic enemy. The creation of a small, weak and ethnically German Austrian state offered no lasting guarantees that Germany might not one day come to offer a new threat to Italy, but for the foreseeable future Germany's enforced weakness and the ban on Austro-German union seemed to cancel out this possibility indefinitely.

If the outcome of the war and the peace settlement appeared to have solved one major problem, in the eyes of many Italians it had created or failed to solve several others. Against the background of the 'mutilated victory' furore, new challenges to Italy's position in the Mediterranean and the Adriatic were posed by the creation of a large Slav state, Yugoslavia, and the advance of an enlarged and ambitious Greece. The latter, together with Britain and France, seemed likelier than Italy to benefit from the disintegration of the Ottoman Empire. In Italy, these developments conflicted both with irredentist claims around the Adriatic and imperialist dreams of African and Middle-Eastern empires.

As a crucial element in Fascism's rise to power, the myth of 'mutilated victory', reinforced by the wider situation throughout what Italian patriots liked to think was their country's 'sphere of interest', was certain to form a central theme of Mussolini's foreign policy. It is true that in this as in other fields fascism's original 1919 programme, tinged as it was with socialism and democracy, gave little sign of what lay ahead. Imperialism was expressly repudiated and while Italy's Adriatic claims were clearly affirmed, so was the new movement's commitment to pursuing them legally and peacefully. Such fine words, like most of those in early fascism's pronouncements, proved to have little staying power. As the movement itself underwent transformation, so did its foreign policy perspectives. The vast influx of active recruits to the *fasci* and the PNF between 1920 and 1922 included large numbers of ultra-patriotic war veterans whose views demanded recognition. For many, D'Annunzio's exploits at Fiume exemplified the kind of uncomplicated approach to the pursuit of Italian interests they admired, and there is no question that the poet-hero gave fascism, and Mussolini in particular, a great deal to live up to. After the March on Rome Fascism's already much changed ethos was further reinforced by the absorption of Nationalists and other conservatives. The Nationalists' conception of Italy's international role was aptly expressed by Luigi Federzoni, in words his new leader would have been happy to use: 'We Italians like to be loved, but prefer to be envied and feared.' Henceforth all the main Fascist factions – ex-Nationalists, ex-syndicalists, modernizing technocrats and former *squadristi* – advocated a 'revisionist' foreign policy aimed at modifying in Italy's favour a peace settlement deemed insulting to its status as a victor and a great power.

There is no reason to believe that Mussolini's views by now differed from these. Among the influences which had obliterated his socialism were at least two favourable not only to a revisionist policy but also to the use of force in pursuing it. The first of these was the pseudo-Darwinian belief in perpetual international struggle held (for somewhat different reasons) both by Nationalists and by many ex-syndicalists, and directed chiefly against 'decadent' France. The second, which soon began to find its way into Fascist iconography and visual propaganda, was the Futurists' exaltation of modern technology, weaponry and war. The resultant cocktail was a dangerously intoxicating one, especially when supped by someone as vain, capricious, violent and authoritarian in temperament as Mussolini. While it may therefore be misleading to speak of a coherently conceived and consistently pursued revisionist foreign policy or of a 'plan' for imperial conquest, two things may be confidently suggested. First, there can be little doubt that revisionism did constitute the prime inspiration for Mussolini's behaviour in the international arena. Second, Mussolini as an individual was not only disposed towards the use of force if he thought he could get away with it but actually considered it good for the nation's collective health.

This conclusion is strengthened by two further ingredients: the perennially hard-to-contain and therefore vital-to-channel violence that was intrinsic both to Fascism's collective psychology and to its totalitarian thrust; and the ostentatiously militaristic character of Mussolini's domestic policies, so many of which, significantly, were depicted in terms of 'battle'. Fascism's 'battle for births' aimed, by encouraging large families, to boost Italy's population chiefly in order to provide her armed forces with manpower and justify demands for more territory. The purpose of the 'battle for grain' was to make Italy self-sufficient in the most important of all basic foodstuffs so that this rising population, steeped in militaristic values and quasi-military disciplines by Fascist education and Fascist propaganda, could be adequately fed in times of war. And Fascist industrial policy, as we have seen, sacrificed export industry in favour of the heavy industry necessary to war production. These were not the policies of a regime, or of a leader, likely to settle for lasting peace.

Mussolini's diplomacy, 1922–32

Whatever Mussolini's inclination, during the 1920s the complete domination of Europe by France and Britain precluded not only an aggressively revisionist foreign policy but also the kind of precarious international equilibrium that might permit Italy to enjoy the diplomatic importance of a potential upsetter. The Duce accordingly restricted himself to mostly rhetorical defiance of the post-war status quo, coupled somewhat contradictorily with the pursuit, which he was never wholeheartedly to abandon, of acceptance as a 'respectable' statesman of continental or even world stature, capable of obtaining gains for Italy through skilful diplomacy. The Duce nevertheless remained restless. His scorn for Anglo-French democracy and League of Nations pacifism was genuinely felt, openly and frequently expressed, and – especially from his position of national leadership – aggravated by an intense jealousy of French and British power. France's African empire, its diplomatic web in south-eastern Europe, its possession of Corsica, Nice and Tunis, and its harbouring of *Giustizia e Libertà* and other Italian anti-fascist émigrés aroused in him a rage that allowed little qualification. Towards Britain his resentment at a Mediterranean presence based on possession of Gibraltar, Malta and Suez, was mixed with reluctant admiration. It was an ambivalence he shared with his eventual ally, Adolf Hitler.

Mussolini's first year as prime minister of Italy revealed both of his faces as an international actor: that of the adventurer and that of the statesman-diplomatist. A combination of boldness and negotiation enabled him to better D'Annunzio and actually achieve Fiume's incorporation in Italy. The terms of Mussolini's agreement with Yugoslavia were illuminating for Italians not blinded by patriotic zeal: Fiume may have been severed from its Slavic hinterland and condemned to economic stagnation, but Fascists and others delirious at the Italian town's 'redemption' preferred to ignore such uncomfortable details. Less successful was Mussolini's impetuous occupation of the Greek, once Venetian, island of Corfu, which international and especially British pressure forced him to evacuate. Having learned from this embarrassment that he could not yet defy those more powerful than himself, Mussolini for almost a decade trod more warily, seeking to strengthen Italy's position through maintaining good relations with Britain while working to undermine France's alliance system in south-eastern Europe. Crucial to this strategy was his friendly relationship with the British foreign secretary Austen Chamberlain, one of the many European conservatives who admired the Duce's anti-bolshevism and imposition of internal 'order'. Chamberlain's benevolence ensured British acquiescence in the establishment of an Italian protectorate over Albania in 1926 and made possible the cession to Italy of two small pieces of African territory.

Italy's interests in both Africa and the Balkans remained very much alive and were pursued by Mussolini in ways not always entirely 'respectable'. The Albanian protectorate, especially given the turbulent nation's location between Yugoslavia and Greece, was merely one way of extending Italian influence in south-eastern Europe; others included the encouragement of subversive movements, especially among Yugoslavia's various minorities, and the signing in 1927 of a treaty with another revisionist state under right-wing rule, the Hungary of Admiral Miklós Horthy. The goal of such activities was the replacement of French by Italian influence in the Balkans and the fulfilment of Italian claims around the Adriatic, if necessary through the dismemberment of Yugoslavia. In Africa Fascist policies between 1922 and 1932 were epitomized by the utterly ruthless subjection of the Arab and Berber population of Libya and the signing in 1928 of a treaty of 'friendship' with Ethiopia. The events of the next decade were to teach both Ethiopians and Albanians that Mussolini's notions of 'friendship' and 'protection' were very much his own.

By the late 1920s Mussolini's impatience with formal diplomacy was rising – in part, perhaps, because of the disrespectful attitude displayed towards his diplomatic posturings by uncensored foreign journalists and cartoonists. His language on international issues was becoming more strident, and from 1928 'revisionism' was declared official policy. Prudence nevertheless remained necessary in practice. For all the Duce's hyperbolic – or, to put it another way, lying – oratory concerning his reborn country's supposedly 5-million-strong, swiftly mobilizable army and its air force capable of 'blotting out the sun', Italy was still poorly prepared for serious military conflict. The onset of the depression in 1929 made things worse; at a time when he would have preferred lavish expenditure on the armed forces, Mussolini had no choice but to accept deep cuts in the military budget; the result was another three years' enforced diplomatic caution. It was this, rather than any underlying shift of policy or the moderation of Grandi as foreign secretary, that inspired the latter's support in this period for general disarmament and the League of Nations.

July 1932 marked a turning point. In that month Mussolini resumed the foreign secretaryship and proceeded to fill important foreign office posts with committed Fascists. Earlier tactical ambivalence was now largely abandoned, and policies clearly perceptible from the late 1920s were intensified. The Duce had become deeply frustrated at what seemed the sparse achievements of his relative diplomatic propriety. Negotiation over Africa and diplomatic manoeuvring in the Balkans were coming to seem less appealing and glorious than terrorism and imperialism. Other considerations doubtless pushed him in the same direction. At home the PNF had lost its political role and the corporativist experiment (thanks in no small way to the Duce's apathy in the matter) was running out of steam, yet Fascism's 'revolutionary' appetite still demanded nourishment; relations with the Vatican had stabilized; in Italy's existing colonies resistance had been crushed; and in Europe the era of Anglo-French monopoly was drawing to a close. The Duce, who a decade earlier had assured foreigners that 'Fascism is not for export', now increasingly laid claim to an ideological conception of foreign policy: this was to be the era of Fascism, in which Italy's imperial destiny would be fulfilled at last.

Realizing the imperial dream: Ethiopia, 1932–6

Hitler's assumption of the German chancellorship in January 1933 transformed the European scene. What this would eventually mean for Mussolini, Fascism and Italy could not have been predicted, especially since Mussolini had until quite recently been dismissive of Nazism.

Although flattered by the rise to power in Germany of a man who openly venerated him, the Duce could not be entirely comfortable with the new situation. On the one hand the re-entry of a nationalistic Germany to the international stage could be expected to make the British, and still more the French, take Italy more seriously. On the other hand a nationalistic Germany might come to challenge Mussolini's own ambitions and even threaten the integrity of Italy itself. Hitler's known designs on Austria, where the local brand of Nazism was also rapidly gaining strength, raised the spectre of a revival, but in far more menacing form, of the threat to Italy's north-eastern frontier once posed by Austria-Hungary. The fact that in 1919 this frontier had advanced to enclose a substantial German-speaking minority only increased Italy's potential vulnerability to a new Germany with strong views on German ethnicity. It was to ward off such dangers that Mussolini had for some time been sponsoring the *Heimwehr*, Austria's homegrown fascists, and in 1934 supported the authoritarian Catholic regime of the Austrian chancellor, Engelbert Dollfuss. In July 1934, when Austrian Nazis launched an unsuccessful *putsch* and assassinated Dollfuss, Mussolini moved troops to the Austrian frontier as a warning to Germany. Hitler had absolutely no intention of intervening at this stage, but the move boosted both Mussolini's morale and his standing at home and abroad.

The Duce's hopes of exploiting the new continental balance in order to become the arbiter of Europe were frustrated during 1933–4 by British and French resistance. He was nevertheless correct in anticipating that Britain and France would allow him greater freedom of action in another area which was increasingly preoccupying him: East Africa. Italy's failure to establish a major East African empire in the late nineteenth century, climaxed by the humiliation of Adowa in 1896, represented for devotees of Italy's supposed 'imperial destiny' a stain on the nation's honour that sooner or later must be expunged. This could only be achieved at the expense of Ethiopia, now Africa's sole surviving independent, indigenously ruled state. Since the PNF's absorption in 1923 of the Nationalists, with their strong attachment to – and eloquent articulation of – the idea of empire, most active Fascists had embraced imperialist values. Official propaganda increasingly linked the imperial glories of Rome with a grandiose Italian future. Mussolini, notwithstanding his constitutional subordination to the Crown and the ambiguous models provided by so many Roman emperors, was certainly not averse, as the 1930s advanced, to attempts by toadies like Starace to portray him in 'imperial' terms. As for the army, while many officers had their reservations about aspects of Fascism and were well aware of Italy's continuing military limitations, the prospect of an easy if overdue revenge over a weak African enemy could be expected to keep them in line.

The initial planning for a military annexation of Ethiopia took place in the ministry for Colonies, on Mussolini's direct orders, towards the end of 1932. The Duce's decision to move towards annexation coincided – almost certainly *not* coincidentally – with the tenth anniversary of the March on Rome, the end of the brutal Libyan 'pacification', and the start of Weimar Germany's final crisis. The army was drawn into the planning process a few months later. In December 1934 the nation's military and civilian elites were informed of the Duce's decision to invade, and what was to be a ten-month crisis began with a convenient 'incident' at Wal-Wal, an oasis on the border between Italian Somaliland and Ethiopia. Wal-Wal having enabled him to raise the level of tension, Mussolini proceeded to spurn suggestions of mediation in the confident expectation that France and Britain would treat him understandingly. He was not disappointed. At the Stresa conference of April 1935, involving Italy, France and Britain and convened in response to German 'revisionism', the French and British studiously avoided any mention of Ethiopia; later in the year Britain went so far (further indeed than it had any right to do) as to 'offer' Mussolini a slice of Ethiopian territory. Only war would now satisfy Mussolini, however. The empire, he declared, 'cannot be made in any other way'. On 3 October 1935 war began. Anglo-French generosity still had one card to play: the Hoare-Laval pact, intended to offer Mussolini enough of Ethiopia to ensure his control over the rump state that would have remained. Outraged public opinion in Britain forced the scheme's withdrawal before Mussolini's response was known. Meanwhile the League of Nations had voted for economic sanctions against Italy. These proved a farce; the vital commodity of oil was not included, the British refrained from closing the Suez Canal to Italian shipping, and no sanctions were imposed by nations such as Germany and the United States who were not League members. By May 1936 the war was over and Italy's east African empire was at last a reality. Vittorio Emanuele III was proclaimed emperor of the last substantial territory to succumb to European imperialism. Mussolini and the Fascist regime had reached their pinnacle of success. They were to rise no higher.

The conquest of Ethiopia represented Mussolini's accomplishment of what had been an Italian nationalist dream for half a century.

However, neither the problems of the depression nor the African interests of certain industrial pressure groups were sufficient to dictate it. It is undeniable that war-related industries profited from the war itself, and more varied sectors of the economy from the subsequent demands of colonial construction. None of this *drove* imperialism, however. To a limited degree and very much in the short term, victory and a new colony may have seemed to vindicate the well-worn, Nationalist-derived propaganda with which the Fascist regime justified its expansionism. Belief in such blessings as abundant land for emigrant settlement, cheap and plentiful raw materials and new markets for Italian manufactures: this may indeed have gripped both Fascist militants and a wider Italian public. Yet existing colonies, notably Libya, were already failing to attract the millions of potential emigrants beloved of Fascist propaganda, and were proving unrewarding to the few thousand who actually settled there; moreover, their administration, policing and economic infrastructures constituted a considerable drain on the Italian treasury. Either way, it is difficult to accept that such considerations somehow *pushed* Italy into war or even weighed heavily where it really mattered: in the mind of Benito Mussolini. Had it done so he would soon have had reason for second thoughts that actually, so far as we know, never troubled him. The acquisition of Ethiopia, as might easily have been predicted, was soon to prove a disappointment as great as that of Libya.

The explanation for the attack on Ethiopia is fundamentally a simple one, to be found in Fascism itself, its Duce, and the relationship between them. The Fascist need for excitement, conflict and dramatic success was one of the movement's truly essential characteristics. Mussolini's recognition and quite self-conscious incarnation of this *machismo* was further sanctified by the successful absurdities of the cult that surrounded him. Most of this was alien to, or at most an optional and easily disposable 'extra' for, other, far more durable, southern European dictatorships. Franco in Spain and Salazar in Portugal constructed personal cults on the appeal of stability and sheer *lack* of excitement. Neither Mussolini's individual psychology nor the collective psychology of Fascism rendered such a future conceivable – fatally, in the end, for both.

7

The decline and fall of Fascism, 1936–45

The Duce at war, 1936–43

With the conquest of Ethiopia accomplished, Mussolini stood at a diplomatic crossroads. Whatever methods he may now have begun to use, as far as his goals were concerned he had not yet ventured beyond the well-worn paths of Italian foreign policy. Despite British support of sanctions over Ethiopia, those ties with Britain which had formed the most consistent element in his diplomacy remained intact. The Duce's horizons were shifting, however, and within weeks, with his acquiescent son-in-law Ciano at the foreign ministry, he had embarked on a course that was entirely new. In July 1936 right-wing military and civilian rebels rose against the elected government of the Spanish Republic. Mussolini, who had been funding Spanish right-wing militias since 1934, saw the rebellion as an opportunity to help kill off democracy and 'bolshevism' in a leading Latin sister-state while also extending Italian influence throughout the western Mediterranean. Anticipating another quick and easy victory on top of that in Ethiopia, he accordingly threw Italian resources into the war on the rebel side. It was to be a major investment: 25,000 troops and Fascist militiamen at the peak in 1937 and over 70,000 in all, together with quantities of aircraft, weapons and ammunition that Italy could ill afford to squander. Victory, moreover, proved far from quick and easy: the Spanish Civil War dragged on for almost three years before the rebel

Nationalists, under their leader Franco, finally overcame Republican resistance on 31 March 1939. The war, while advertising the impressive military professionalism of Franco's other principal foreign patron, Nazi Germany, exposed and aggravated Italy's military deficiencies. As for the expected rewards, here too Italy, while obtaining some strategic benefit, was smoothly upstaged by its German ally. The conduct of Italian troops and militia over the course of the war was at best uneven. The defeat of Italian Fascist forces at the battle of Guadalajara (March 1937) acquired special significance. Inflicted in part by the Garibaldi battalion of the volunteer International Brigades, made up of Italian anti-fascist exiles, it provided anti-fascists within Italy with a double reassurance: that the flame of resistance still burned, and that the power of Fascism was not insuperable. For any Italian Fascists who were prepared to replace sloganizing with analysis, the Spanish experience offered evidence that the transformation of Italians into 'new Fascist men' still had some way to go.

Mussolini's Spanish adventure demonstrated conclusively the new ideological and expansionist direction of his foreign policy. The 'decadent' democracies, the Duce now declared, must learn that this was the 'century of Fascism' and that the Mediterranean, in terms of influence at least, was an 'Italian lake'. This risky new course was wholly of Mussolini's own choosing, for the democracies themselves, France and Britain, showed little wish to alienate someone whose friendship in the face of a resurgent Germany they were anxious to maintain. It was precisely this resurgence, however, epitomized for Mussolini by Hitler's re-militarization of the Rhineland in March 1936, that convinced him his diplomatic future lay with Germany. In October 1936, buoyed up by their partnership in Spain, the two powers concluded on Mussolini's initiative a loose association to which the Duce gave the name 'Axis'. The forming of the Rome-Berlin Axis marked the first step in what was to prove a fateful relationship. The die was cast in 1938 with Mussolini's adoption of a neutral stance over Germany's annexation of Austria, the *Anschluss*. The contrast with his anti-German belligerence in 1934 was striking, and from this point onward the relative positions of the two dictators were reversed. Mussolini, initially somewhat condescending towards his less experienced fellow-dictator, was bedazzled by German military strength during a visit in September 1937. By the time of the *Anschluss* he was becoming indisputably the lesser figure and Italy the junior partner in the new relationship. Subsequent events merely underlined Italy's subaltern status. At the October 1938 Munich conference, Mussolini, attempting yet again to pose as arbiter of Europe, was visibly a peripheral figure. Germany's diplomatic success at Munich and Hitler's completion of Czechoslovakia's destruction early in 1939 stung an admiring but jealous Mussolini into a blatant and pathetic act of emulation: the formal annexation in April 1939 of Italy's Albanian 'protectorate'. In May 1939 an increasingly uneasy and unhappy Ciano was pushed by his father-in-law into signing with Germany a new agreement, the Pact of Steel. Unlike the loose and unspecific Axis arrangement, the Pact of Steel was an unambiguously military alliance, drafted according to German wishes and committing the two states to mutual assistance in the event of any, and not merely defensive, hostilities.

This did not mean that Italy was ready in mid-1939 for the kind of war into which the German alliance seemed likely to pull it. When the Germans had first suggested a firm military alliance, in May 1938, Mussolini had demurred on the grounds partly that Italian public opinion was unprepared and partly that Italy would be militarily unready for hostilities against major powers (whichever they might be) before 1942. Now that the pact existed, but with Italian military and economic resources stretched in East Africa, squandered in Spain and diluted in Albania, he declared that it would be 1943 before his country could play its part. Coming from a dictator whose dream had been to transform his country into a warrior nation, and who had had almost seventeen years in which to make that dream reality, this was hardly an affirmation of success.

However embarrassing, Mussolini's appraisal of Italy's state of military preparedness was also an essentially sound one, and showed that he was far from having lost all grip on reality. The events of 1939–43 showed how right he was to be cautious in 1938–9 and how wrong he later was to ignore his own warning voice. On the outbreak of war in September 1939 he disingenuously asked Hitler for impossible quantities of arms and raw materials as the price of Italy's immediate participation, receiving instead – as he surely intended – the Führer's acceptance of Italian neutrality. In spring 1940, however, as the Germans swept across north-western Europe, the Duce, uneasy at cutting so unheroic a figure in such stirring times, decided to throw Italy into what now looked like being a short war; only thus could Italy hope to attain its full Mediterranean and Balkan destiny.

Once again, as with Spain in 1936, Mussolini's 'short, victorious war' calculations hit wide of the mark. His pre-war assessment of Italy's military potential, on the other hand, proved shamingly accurate. From the outset Italy's war went badly. Minuscule advances into south-eastern France in June 1940 were followed in October by a disastrously unsuccessful invasion of Greece from which Italy was rescued only by German intervention. In North Africa, the principal sphere allotted by Germany to Italian arms, early advances were rolled back by the British during late 1940 and effective command assumed during 1941 by the Germans under General Rommel. Meanwhile, by mid-1941 Italy's recently-won East African empire had been overrun by the British. By now, though, Mussolini's commitment to Hitler was total. In summer 1941 it inspired him, quite unnecessarily, to send Italian forces to assist in Germany's invasion of the Soviet Union. Even more foolishly, he followed this in December, after the Japanese attack on Pearl Harbor, with the ultimate and suicidal absurdity of declaring war on the United States. When the tide of war in Europe and North Africa began to turn against the Axis during 1942, it was Fascist Italy, far more than its German ally, that stood exposed to the western Allies' counter-offensive. This began in November 1942 with the Axis collapse at El Alamein and the Anglo-American invasion of French North Africa. Six months later the Axis forces in North Africa were crushed and on 9 July 1943 Allied troops, with the connivance of a re-emerging Mafia, landed in Sicily. The ultimate test of Fascism was about to begin.

The overthrow of Mussolini

In May 1936, with his regime firmly established and Italy's place in the African sun apparently secure, Mussolini's standing with his fellow Italians was at its peak. Thereafter, although this may not have been evident on a day-to-day basis, it entered a more or less steady decline. Fittingly, the downturn began with Italy's illegal intervention in Spain, an undertaking that was unpopular from the outset and all the more so the longer it dragged on. Every bit as important was Italy's increasing closeness and subservience to Nazi Germany. The demeaning nature of Italy's position *vis-à-vis* Germany was thrown into sharp relief in 1938 by the unresisted arrival of Germany's looming presence on the Brenner frontier. Many Italians were also repelled by the clearly related signs of radicalization within the Fascist regime, especially the 1938 racial laws, introduced in what looked like slavish imitation of Nazi racism. Among those who found Mussolini's new course distasteful was the king, whose enjoyment of imperial status was soured by his distaste at Italy's increasing deference to Germany. Quite apart from his personal dislike of Hitler – which was fully reciprocated – Vittorio

Emanuele had every reason to be suspicious of the Führer's influence over the Duce. By the late 1930s the one-time republican Mussolini, envious of Hitler's complete dominance within Germany and impatient with his own constitutional subjection to the Crown, was gripped by a renewed desire to undermine the monarchy's position. The Duce's assumption of command over the armed forces in 1940 further antagonized a monarch who, as the war went on and the news got worse, grew less inclined to accept Mussolini's indispensability.

A key source of pre-war anti-Germanism among Italians was the general and legitimate fear of embroilment in German-instigated hostilities against other major powers. In June 1940, nevertheless, Italian public opinion rallied, somewhat reluctantly and with little sign of real enthusiasm, behind the regime. Probably it is not too cynical to suggest that had Italy's war prospered, Mussolini would have reaped new glory and popularity. Instead, the succession of Italian defeats simply laid bare the emptiness of his bellicose bombast and the all-round shortcomings of Fascism as a system. As Italian forces struggled, German influence grew ever greater, not only in the war zone but also within Italy itself. Loss of 'imperial' territory in North and East Africa, combined with heavy Italian casualties in Russia, encouraged both conservative fellow-travellers and pragmatic Fascists to seek a way out of the German alliance and a separate peace with the Allies. Italy's domestic condition strengthened such desires, with acute shortages of food and other essentials and, in March 1943, a renewal of major strike activity in northern Italy's industrial districts.

At this point, early in 1943, Mussolini precipitated the crisis of his own regime. The Duce was now a sick man, plagued by acute gastric troubles which were no less debilitating for being, it seems likely, at least partly psychosomatic. No longer an impressive figure and looking older than his sixty years, he was losing the respect of many leading Fascists. Perhaps sensing this and gnawed by unfamiliar feelings of vulnerability, he surrounded himself with yes-men and ignored the flagrant corruption of Party hacks and the numerous relatives of his mistress, Clara Petacci. Between February and April 1943 the Duce demoted several of Fascism's leading figures, among them Ciano, Bottai and Grandi. The effect was to throw these influential and now disgruntled Fascists into the arms of anti-German – and therefore anti-Mussolini – conspirators: a motley collection of well-heeled monarchists, resurfacing liberal politicians, important figures within the military and police, and moderate Fascist dissidents.

The Anglo-American invasion of Sicily brought matters to a head. On 16 July 1943 the Fascist dissenters succeeded in persuading Mussolini to convene the Fascist Grand Council for what would be its first session since 1939. During the week before the Council assembled, Mussolini's standing with informed and influential Italians slipped still further. On 19 July the Duce met Hitler at Feltre in northern Italy. As was now usual, the Führer dominated both the proceedings and his Italian ally. Mussolini, utterly cowed, shrank from doing what his military and political advisers had been urging him to do: telling Hitler that Italy could not continue fighting.

The fateful meeting of the Fascist Grand Council opened on 24 July 1943, lasted through the night, and saw Mussolini under criticism from not one side but two. On one flank stood Grandi, Ciano, Bottai and what might be termed the 'moderates', who wished to break with Germany and accepted that this would require Mussolini's removal. For some, this was the only way not merely of rescuing Italy from German clutches, but also Fascism from those of an alien Nazism; others were prepared to see Fascism disappear in the wider and longer-term interests of Italy. On the other flank stood those councillors whose hopes lay in precisely the opposite direction. For the embittered Farinacci and other diehards, radicals and pro-Germans, a further tightening of the German alliance must be combined with a revitalized, 'nazified' Party revolution at home. The diehards were to have their chance later, but for now the 'moderates' were in the majority. After much discussion a motion proposed by Grandi, one of Mussolini's longest-standing Fascist comrades, passed comfortably. Calling for the king to resume command of the armed forces of Italy, it amounted to a vote of no confidence in the Duce's leadership. Mussolini, appearing less distressed than some of those who after two decades of hero-worship had voted against him, left the meeting refusing to believe that this tame, 'consultative' body could harm him. He was mistaken. On 25 July 1943, the king, informed of the Council's vote, seized the opportunity to invoke a constitutional power that had lain all but dormant since the Matteotti crisis nineteen years earlier. At an interview with Mussolini, Vittorio Emanuele informed the man who had made him an emperor that he was no longer prime minister of Italy. As the bewildered Mussolini left the royal presence he was courteously arrested.

The Republic of Salò and the end of Fascism

On Mussolini's fall the king entrusted the premiership to a monarchist general, Badoglio, and the way was prepared for Italy's surrender to the Allies. This came on 8 September 1943, and was followed in October by the Kingdom of Italy's declaration of war on its recent Axis partner, Germany. Changing sides part-way through a war which quite clearly still had a long way to go was an inevitably difficult business. When the Allies landed on the southern Italian mainland near Salerno in early September 1943, the Germans responded by formally occupying the north and centre of the country. For the next twenty months Italy was the stage for two overlapping wars: a conventional struggle between the slowly advancing Allies and the Germans, and an intensifying, bitter civil war between Italian Fascist diehards and the fast-growing Resistance.

The absence of any popular opposition to Mussolini's overthrow, the meagreness of Fascist opposition to the Allies and the virtual evaporation of Fascist organization in those Italian regions not under German military control, provided stark testimony to the limitations of Fascism's achievement. During 1943, it became clear that Fascism had failed not only to construct an authentic and enduring new state, but also to sink roots deep into Italian society, transform Italian culture and create a reborn Italian people driven by heroic, martial and self-sacrificial values. In so far as such values certainly *did* exist among Italians, they were proving far less likely to surface in the service of Fascism than in pursuit of its extinction. None of this was contradicted, even if the scenery on the stage was somewhat altered, by the new version of Fascism which soon appeared within the German-occupied zone. The Germans were anxious to bolster their military position in Italy by propping up Fascism in the areas they controlled and ensuring the continued obedience of the civil population. For these purposes they needed the services of Mussolini, who following his arrest was under detention at Gran Sasso, high in the Apennine mountains. On 12 September 1943 German paratroopers accordingly carried out an audacious act of rescue. The Duce, miraculously liberated and now bound to Hitler by a debt of gratitude, was borne northwards by his rescuers to a new role: that of head of a new Fascist 'state', the suggestively named Italian Social Republic (*Repubblìca Sociale Italiana*: RSI). While the new republic claimed power over all of Italy, its actual boundaries were those of the German-occupied zone and were to contract as it contracted. In clear expectation of further retreat its administrative centres were established as far from the encroaching battlefront as possible. Appropriately for a regime whose content was to be more propagandistic than practical, it was the location of its propaganda headquarters, the town of Salò on the banks of Lake Garda, that gave it its more commonly used title: the Republic of Salò.

Superficially the RSI represented a reversion to that early fascist social radicalism which had been progressively marginalized, first in the quest for power and then in its consolidation. The RSI's ruling personnel consisted mostly of second-rank – and second-rate – figures and hitherto frustrated radical Fascists; its programme, defined at the Congress of Verona in November 1943, was rabidly republican – understandably in view of the king's dismissal of Mussolini – and anti-Semitic, and while guaranteeing private property rights, envisaged both land reform and the involvement of workers and the state in the running of industry. This social radicalism, though taken very seriously by its authors – and by many post-war neo-fascists – nevertheless rang hollow. Many Fascists refused to pursue its implementation; industrialists successfully resisted it just as a decade earlier they had evaded the demands of corporativism; workers, increasingly organized by the reviving Communists and Socialists, struck against it; and, crucially, the Germans nullified it. For if in theory the RSI embodied a return to Fascist 'leftism', what it truly laid bare was the Fascist rump state's total subjection to Nazi Germany. While Fascist enthusiasts talked of worker participation in industry, the Germans ruthlessly dispatched Italian workers to labour in Germany; while the nationalist rhetoric of Salò's slick propaganda machine continued unabated, Germany flouted the Pact of Steel by annexing Italian territory won from Austria-Hungary in 1918–19; and all the while the RSI, created by Germans and radical Fascists to keep Italians loyal, presided over the precise opposite as more and more flocked to the Resistance. And if the RSI's programme showed Fascism's most theoretically 'progressive' side, the actions of its militants and its head of state showed Fascism at its most vindictive and vicious. Opposition and resistance were treated with a sadistic brutality that exceeded even the worst acts of *squadrismo*, while Mussolini's 'betrayers' within the Party were vilified and remorselessly pursued. Only one of the leading July 'traitors' were actually caught, however. Count Galeazzo Ciano, one-time foreign secretary, was hastily tried and shot with the approval of his unforgiving father-in-law.

Meanwhile, the area nominally governed by the RSI continued to shrink. The Allies' capture of Rome on 4 June 1944 dealt a massive blow to German and Italian Fascist morale. It was promptly followed by Badoglio's replacement with a civilian-led government which looked forward to the end of war and the rebirth of Italian democracy. By August 1944 the Allies were as far north as Florence, and by the end of the year they controlled all of Italy south of a line from the Ligurian gulf to the Adriatic at Rimini. During early 1945, as Germany itself was invaded from both west and east, the Allies and the ever-burgeoning Resistance swiftly recaptured northern Italy – what might reasonably be regarded as not only Fascism's last bastion but also its principal heartland. With his paper regime in shreds, Mussolini, after an abortive attempt to arrange terms with the Resistance, fled northwards towards the frontier under German protection. Intercepted and seized by the Resistance, the Duce received no mercy. Instead, on 28 April 1945, he and his mistress Clara Petacci were shot dead and their bodies brought back to Milan. There, in the city that had given birth to Fascism some 26 years earlier, the Duce made his final public appearance – as a bedraggled cadaver, suspended upside-down in a city-square petrol station, exposed to the scorn and hatred of the populace.

8

Interpreting Italian Fascism

During its lifetime Italian Fascism aroused intense controversy among politically aware Europeans, especially as it came to be seen as merely the first example of a widespread phenomenon. In present-day Italy controversy continues as neo-fascists and so-called 'post-fascists' venerate Mussolini's memory while left-wing Italians remain unwilling to view Fascism in any but the most negative terms. Among students of Italian Fascism, and of its place in the history of fascism as a wider European phenomenon, numerous interpretations of this elusive period in Italian history struggle for acceptance. The sections which follow consider some of the most important.

Fascism, moral crisis and mass society

Many Italian liberals who witnessed the emergence of Fascism and its rise to power were reluctant to regard it as a deep-rooted or complex movement requiring careful attention and analysis. Nor were they keen to see it as arising out of long-standing, chronic shortcomings within the liberal system to which they adhered. The outstanding exemplar of this tendency was the Neapolitan philosopher and historian Benedetto Croce. Probably the single most important Italian intellectual of his generation, Croce not only lived through the Fascist period but was largely protected by his eminence from censorship and harassment at the hands of the regime. For Croce, Fascism was a symptom and unfortunate by-product of a temporary and therefore reversible moral decline within Italian liberalism. Since the turn of the century, he argued, the liberal 'sense of freedom' had been debased by materialism, exaggerated nationalism, and a growing admiration for 'heroic' figures. The new masses thrust onto the political stage during these years lacked liberal sensibilities and were easily manipulated by a minority of Fascist hooligans, while Italy's governing class had lapsed into corruption and incompetence. Fascism, while able to take advantage of this sad but redeemable situation, was thus an interruption in Italy's achievement of ever greater 'freedom', a short-term moral infection from which Italy, by re-dedicating itself to the ideal of freedom, could just as quickly recover. Ironically, Fascist intellectuals and propagandists agreed with Croce concerning the moral degeneracy of liberalism; where they differed was in seeing liberalism as *intrinsically* flawed, and Fascism as not so much a symptom as the cure.

In placing emphasis on the weaknesses and faults of Italian liberalism and the moral fragility of its leading exponents, Croce set a course that continued to appeal to many non-Italians who viewed Mussolini as a mere opportunist and Fascism as an inherently shallow phenomenon unworthy of prolonged and serious analysis. An outstanding example, though one with a very different perception of Italian liberalism from Croce's, is the distinguished British historian of modern Italy and biographer of Mussolini, Denis Mack Smith. For Mack Smith, along with many Anglo-American scholars who disagree with him on other points, the weaknesses in Italian liberalism which gave Fascism its opportunity were not, as Croce believed, a temporary intrusion but were inherent in the Risorgimento and the system it spawned. As this brief study has suggested, it is undeniable that Italian liberalism's shortcomings did make a major contribution to Fascism's appearance, growth and conquest of power. That these shortcomings were as recent as Croce suggested, and the liberal 'sense of freedom' previously so central an element of Italian life, is highly questionable. Mack Smith and others are surely right to insist that the problems of liberalism, whether or not they were 'moral', were not ephemeral but chronic. The reluctance of Crocean liberals (a more or less extinct breed today) and of more recent, in other respects very different, liberal scholars to take Fascism's sociological and ideological significance seriously is another matter entirely.

Croce's identification of illiberal and manipulable 'masses' as a problem for Italian liberalism may be said to have linked him with an approach to the understanding of Fascism which continued to win adherents for many years, even decades after its original emergence. Down, certainly, until the 1970s, a variety of scholars, mainly social scientists, attempted to explain Fascism in terms of the arrival on the political scene of what were often termed 'amorphous masses'. Rapid industrialization, urbanization, war and demobilization, they suggested, tore millions of Italians from their traditional roots and destroyed their customary local, personal, socio-economic and cultural relationships. Powerless and directionless, these abandoned souls fell prey to skilful demagogues and well-organized minorities who were able to use them to challenge the dominance of ruling elites. This view of Fascism, like Croce's, owed much to the work of early twentieth-century elitist writers like Pareto, Mosca and Michels, and was in part shared by many Fascist intellectuals and propagandists. For them, of course, the conclusions were entirely different, and Fascism's role in relation to the supposedly 'amorphous masses' wholly positive. Eager to decry the 'old' liberal regime and its 'political class' for their remoteness from the Italian people, Fascists pointed to their own movement's mass appeal while denying its connection with any particular social class or classes. Fascism, in the eyes of its devotees, restored a sense of identity and community to countless individuals alienated from each other by rapid socio-economic changes.

A related approach to that of 'mass society' theorists was adopted during the inter-war period by psychologists such as Erich Fromm and Wilhelm Reich, who employed their respective versions of Freudian psychoanalytical theory to explain the susceptibility of individuals and masses to the appeal of Fascism. It hardly needs to be said that this categorization of Fascism as, in effect, a kind of psychopathological disorder, was definitely *not* congenial to actual Fascists. Between the 1960s and the 1980s a related brand of analysis was adopted by a school of self-styled 'psycho-historians', though for the time being at least the vogue, which was always fuelled chiefly by an interest in Nazism, appears to have run its course.

Given the explosive arrival of 'mass politics' in Italy between 1912 and 1922, it is clear that Italian Fascism's rapid rise *was* related to the kinds of changes referred to above, and to the failure of existing political parties to embrace and represent the new forces created by them. Clearly, too, a reliable understanding of the psychological forces driving individual Fascists – whether leaders, activists or mere followers – is valuable if and when we can acquire it. What remain unconvincing in most 'mass society' approaches to Fascism – which tend in any case to be unduly influenced by the case of Germany – are the notions, first, that the new masses were predominantly 'amorphous', irrational, essentially passive and therefore merely manipulated, and, second, that Fascism can somehow be conveniently diagnosed as a mass psychological disorder. Historians, after all, must construct their arguments on firm foundations of empirical research – and the abundant historical evidence accumulated since the 1960s strongly suggests that, at any rate in the Italian case, the great majority of those who, at one level or another, embraced Fascism did so as the result of reasoned – which is not of course to say correct – assessment of their interests and often a strong sense of class or group identification.

Fascism, capitalism and class

An important and enduring thrust within the study and analysis of fascism, in both its specific Italian and its wider, 'generic' form, has insisted upon its connection with the capitalist financial and economic system and the class conflicts it generates. In the 1920s and 1930s, European Marxists, especially those who followed the leadership of Moscow, produced a succession of analyses of fascism, all of which argued that it was in origin the creation of powerful capitalist interests and that when in power it was essentially their tool. Italian capitalism, they insisted, was by the early 1920s incapable of further expansion and therefore created Italian Fascism in order to repress the working class and impose a static, protected economy on Italy. In so far as such interpretations concerned themselves with Fascism's popular support, it was largely to dismiss it as consisting of a lower middle class or 'petty bourgeoisie'. Subjectively crushed between capitalism and organized labour, and objectively doomed to extinction through 'proletarianization', the fearful, downwardly mobile members of this social layer flocked to Fascism for what, even if they did not realize it, could only be temporary protection against historical inevitability.

As has been shown, a close relationship certainly did exist between the Fascist regime and Italy's financial, industrial and agrarian capitalists. Indeed, it is probably not going too far to suggest that without their assistance the original *fasci* would not have recovered from their early failures, and that the Fascist regime would therefore never have been born. The inter-war orthodox Marxist account was nevertheless flawed in several respects – as perceptive Italian Communists such as Antonio Gramsci and Palmiro Togliatti recognized. First, it ignored or at best misunderstood the importance of Fascism's mass following and its emergence independently of capitalist interests. Second, it failed adequately to explain why, in this particular context, capitalists chose to maintain with an unpredictable force like Fascism an alliance whose character was *political* and not just instrumental, rather than settling politically for a liberalism which, when all was said and done, remained firmly pro-capitalist. Third, it exaggerated the importance of such interests in the formulation of policy within the Fascist state. While their influence upon financial and economic policy was very real, once the dictatorship was in place it seldom *determined* it, operating rather through a complex dialectic with regime forces. As for the increasingly crucial sphere of foreign policy, where according to orthodox Marxists the needs of capitalism should have been decisive, it was probably here that its influence was at its lowest. Finally, orthodox Marxism's depiction of a static or contracting economy under Fascism was simply inaccurate, for while it is certainly possible to overstate Italian Fascism's expansionist success, it would also be inaccurate to disregard or dismiss it completely. Gramsci and Togliatti did not, of course, suggest throwing out the baby with the bathwater. Fascism's relationship with capitalism certainly existed and needs to be emphasized, but took subtler forms than Stalinist orthodoxy allowed: forms that required careful analysis and a willingness to take seriously the Fascist allegiances of different social groups.

While it is certainly not necessary to be a Marxist to see 'class' as a helpful concept in understanding Italian Fascism, having once been a Marxist may have a part to play. Between the early 1960s and his death in 1996 the Italian historian Renzo De Felice, a Communist Party member in his early adulthood, produced a substantial body of work on Fascism, most notably a monumental, multi-volume biography of Mussolini. In the process De Felice offered an interpretation of Fascism that aroused great controversy, especially within Italy itself, where, as already noted, Fascism is a matter not of distant history but of personal recollection and enduring passions. De Felice insisted that Italian Fascism possessed ideological and cultural roots traceable back to the eighteenth-century Enlightenment, and had the right to be treated by historians with as much intellectual respect as liberalism or socialism. He made what for him was a crucial distinction between Fascism as a *movement* and Fascism as a *regime*, arguing that the Fascist movement was primarily one of an 'emerging middle class' thrown up by the economic changes and population movements of the years after 1890. This class was eager to challenge the traditional, liberal political class for power – indeed, to take its place. Its spirit, De Felice asserted, was 'vital', 'optimistic' and creative; its ideologies were the 'rational' ones of productivism and corporativism; it was, in short, a 'revolutionary phenomenon' utterly at variance with the lower middle class as depicted by most Marxists and seen by them as providing Fascism with its main social base. De Felice nevertheless recognized the compromises made by Mussolini in order to win power. The resultant Fascist regime was, he admitted, in many respects a 'conservative regime' against which what he termed 'Fascism as movement' – the revolutionary impulse within Fascism – struggled, with limited success, until the very end. A Fascist regime was not, according to De Felice, an inevitability. Mussolini's conservative allies could have prevented Fascism's accession to power and, indeed, have reinvigorated liberalism, but chose not to do so. None the less, he concluded, a 'totalitarian' threat to these conservative interests persisted and, had the war not put an end to Italian Fascism, might well have been intensified.

De Felice's conclusions concerning the role of an 'emergent middle class' have, on the whole, been more widely accepted (though with varying levels of qualification) by other historians than his views on the Fascist movement's air of optimism and creativity; these, his critics assert, lead him to pay insufficient attention to the negative and brutal side of Fascism, which was at least as prominent. His legacy nevertheless remains a powerful one, having done much to inspire what has come to be labelled 'anti-anti-Fascist' historiography. This phenomenon will be explored below, in the final section of this chapter.

Fascism, totalitarianism and modernization

A once popular approach to Fascism, now resurfacing in changed form after a quarter of a century in the intellectual wilderness, focuses on its relationship with 'totalitarianism'. In its original incarnation, this approach involved regarding Italian Fascism as merely one version of 'totalitarianism', a much broader phenomenon encompassing dictatorships of left as well as right. 'Totalitarianism theory' concentrated on the structure and operation of all allegedly totalitarian regimes, rather than on the distinctly varied movements out of which those regimes grew or the different historical contexts which allowed them power. The original proponents of 'totalitarianism theory' stressed the features allegedly common to totalitarian regimes: the leader and the leadership cult; the single party; the official ideology; the directed economy; and the state's monopoly of information and repressive power. They concluded that the similarities between supposedly different kinds of totalitarian regime greatly outweighed the differences.

The heyday of totalitarianism theory was the early part of the Cold War, from the end of the Second World War down to the early 1960s. During this period the concept of totalitarianism was employed by political scientists, mainly American or at any rate American-based, to highlight the resemblances between the new enemy of western democracy, Soviet and Chinese Communism, and the old enemies, Fascism and National Socialism. In its favour was (and remains) the undeniable fact that for most of the population life under one form of 'totalitarian' regime may be much like life under another. Under both Fascism and Communism, fundamental liberal freedoms – of speech, publication and information, of movement and assembly, of political and trade union activity, etc. – disappear, while the fruits of economic effort and the exercise of power over others are enjoyed disproportionately by minorities: wealthy capitalists and members of the Party hierarchy under Fascism and the latter alone under Communism. Such similarities are not to be lightly brushed aside, especially by those of us who have little or no direct experience of what the absence of liberal freedoms means. That said, the lumping together of all supposedly totalitarian regimes – and the too ready assumption that they actually *were* as 'total' in practice as they claimed and superficially appeared to be – obscured a much more nuanced and questionable set of realities. These were increasingly exposed from around 1960 onwards, as historians began to take over the study of Fascism, Nazism and (somewhat later) Soviet Communism from political scientists. Their dissection both of fascist movements throughout Europe and of fascist and kindred regimes tended to bring out the differences, as well as any similarities, between fascism and communism. In the Italian case especially, historical research, stressing the distribution of power within the regime and Fascism's impact on different areas of Italian society, appeared to reveal how far the Fascist goal of totalitarianism was from actually being accomplished. That picture of Fascism is the one that has broadly been embraced here.

The differences between communist and fascist regimes and even more between the ideas, movements and circumstances out of which they respectively emerged, thus remain evident and important. Even so, the collapse of Soviet and eastern European Communism after 1989 reopened scholarly minds to the possibility that 'totalitarianism' might after all still possess conceptual value, albeit for reasons very different from those that once prevailed. Now, interest in 'totalitarianism' involved a synthesis between the original thesis and the 'antithesis' offered by sceptical historians. In the first place, the manner of Soviet

Communism's collapse indicated serious and ultimately fatal weaknesses behind totalitarian façades and suggested that communist regimes were not, after all, 'more totalitarian' than fascist ones. Another striking post-communist phenomenon was the propensity of some ex-communists to embrace a fascist-style, sometimes racially inspired, authoritarian nationalism. These and other developments redrew scholarly attention to those areas where fascism and communism might be said to have had features in common.

One thread of the 'totalitarianism' thesis managed to survive through its years of unfashionableness. Since the 1970s, some writers on Italian Fascism, including both a non-Marxist majority and a Marxist minority, have chose to view it as related to Italy's economic backwardness and to attempts at its 'modernization'. Comparisons have been made, most notably by the controversial American scholar A.J. Gregor, with other twentieth-century dictatorships seeking – as Gregor claims was the case with Italian Fascism – rapid industrialization of a retarded economy. The most obvious case is that of the Soviet Union under Stalin, which, like Italian Fascism, also controlled labour, held down wages and directed investment into heavy industry. Gregor, highlighting the syndicalist and dissident Marxist threads within Fascism's root system, goes so far as to see the two regimes as related not just functionally but also ideologically.

Scholarly response to the depiction, by Gregor and others, of Fascism as a 'modernizing dictatorship' has been mixed. Although some economic historians believe that in Italy's case the attempt at modernization failed because of Mussolini's deference to 'traditional' economic interests, others consider that Fascism did play some part in 'modernizing' an economy which, for all the development since 1900, was still backward after the 1914–18 war. Supporting the latter view are generalized economic statistics dealing with overall production and investment, the development of 'modern' industrial and agricultural sectors under Fascism, and the 'productivist' thread running through the regime. Its critics have warned, however, against mistaking Fascism's often improvised economic policies for purposefulness; against ignoring both the extent and the character of pre-Fascist industrial development, both of which influenced the shape it assumed under Fascism; and against taking at face value the impressive apparatus of state intervention when private interests continued to benefit from the activities of the IRI and the Corporate State. Whether Italy would have modernized more or less without Fascism we can never know; whether Fascism itself was responsible for such modernization as did occur is problematical; and in any case to view Fascism solely or even primarily in these terms is to pay insufficient attention to both the manner of its emergence and the human cost of its two decades in power.

Fascism, 'political religion' and national 'rebirth'

Ever since political scientists and historians began to examine the nature of Italian Fascism, tensions have existed between two broad interpretative approaches. One, inaugurated perhaps by those American political scientists who so earnestly examined and described the supposed mechanisms of the Corporate State, may be said to have viewed Fascism *in its own terms*, treating with some seriousness both its official ideology and its advertised achievements. The other approach, and that which has mostly preoccupied us so far, has viewed most aspects of Fascism with scepticism: its ideology as incoherent and its domestic accomplishments as superficial.

In one form or another, it is the latter tendency that has dominated the scholarly study of Fascism. Those who have read this study carefully may well conclude that it remains very much alive. Yet it is only proper to acknowledge that over the past two decades this fundamentally negative view of Fascism has been seriously challenged by a new generation of scholars who look at Italian Fascism – and indeed the wider phenomenon of comparative fascism – very differently. Two main intellectual sources for this revisionism may be identified. The first, already introduced, is the work of Renzo De Felice and its rejection of what its devotees consider a prejudiced 'anti-Fascism' as a valid intellectual starting point for studying Mussolini and his regime. The second is the relentless rise since the 1980s of cultural history, the history of ideas, cultural theory and discourse analysis. De Felice's influence among Italian historians of Fascism – several of whom were his students and protégées – has been enormous (though by no means uncontested), and that beyond Italy appreciable. Its overall effect has been to boost what has come to be called the 'anti-anti-Fascist' history of Fascism. This involves accentuating whatever 'idealistic' or self-consciously 'revolutionary' elements it has been possible to discern in Fascism and downgrading as extrinsic to the 'essential' Fascism such inconvenient aspects as the Nazi alliance, racial policies, entry into the Second World War and the personal vagaries of the Duce.

The influence on De Felice's successors of cultural history, with its assimilation of the 'linguistic turn', discourse analysis, post-structuralism, etc., has led them to regard as far more than superficial the cultural, iconographic and propagandistic aspects of Fascism. The distinguished, prolific and influential Italian scholar Emilio Gentile (not to be confused with the Fascist education minister) has argued power-fully and persuasively for what might be considered a new 'totalitarian-ism thesis' based on an understanding of Fascism that is more 'cultural' than 'structural'. Gentile suggests that the Fascist regime, and a signifi-cant proportion of Fascist office-holders, were genuinely driven by the pursuit of totalitarianism and a revolution that would be cultural rather than social. This thrust within Fascism, he insists, must be taken ser-iously, not simply at the level of fantasy and rhetoric but at that of conviction and accomplishment. Fascism, Gentile concludes, *was* totali-tarian in the conviction of its leading echelons and their determination to push through a programme of 'anthropological revolution': a pro-gramme, that is, that would transform Italians' individual and collective mentalities. For its ideological zealots, whom Gentile sees as more numerous, more sincere and more central to Fascism than many previ-ous historians would have cared to believe, Fascism was a veritable 'political religion' in ways that went well beyond mere pseudo-religious ritual.

Gentile's work contributes to and draws strength from a broader re-evaluation of Fascism, viewed comparatively or (to use the commonly accepted jargon) *generically*, that has been under way since around 1990. This represents the latest phase in a never-ending (and never entirely successful) quest by historians and social scientists to arrive at a satisfac-tory *definition* of fascism. The most widely embraced definition since the early 1990s has unquestionably been that of the British historian of ideas Roger Griffin, who identifies fascism – and therefore Italian Fascism – with 'populist ultranationalism' and (more significantly) a desire for national 'rebirth' or *palingenesis*. Griffin's elaboration of fas-cism as thus defined has gained widespread acceptance among scholars, even if not quite perhaps the degree of 'consensus' he has come to claim for it. As a historian of ideas he makes a forceful case for taking Fascism's intellectual history seriously, viewing its ideological core as *essential* to its very nature and, indeed, practice.

The approaches represented by Gentile and Griffin, distinct in themselves yet where Fascism is concerned mutually supportive, may thus be said to reflect a renewed interest in and intellectual respect for Fascism's ideas, ideology, stated purposes and – at least in culturally transforming Italy – achievements. The work of both scholars is weighty and thought-provoking. Gentile forces us to re-evaluate what most scholars had come to regard as the superficiality and meretriciousness of Fascism's achievement. Griffin and other intellectual historians of Fascism require us to look more closely at Fascism's intellectual sources and content, and to consider whether these might not provide the key to a deeper understanding of this challenging phenomenon.

It is necessary, nevertheless, to enter a warning here to those undertaking the study of Fascism and its extraordinary leader: beware of Fascist illusionism. Whatever Fascism was or was not good at, it was extremely successful at creating appearances and then persuading observers to confuse these appearance with reality. Scholarly susceptibility to the idea that Fascist theory generated Fascist practice, and that popular exposure to slick and saturating propaganda promised 'anthropological revolution', is unfortunately assisted by some of the less rigorous forms of fashionable cultural history, especially when these are accompanied by neglect of the tougher demands presented by social history. The latter, where still practised, continues to indicate that Fascism was both much more and much less than it claimed to be.

Conclusion

As the volume of serious historical literature on the different aspects of Italian Fascism increases, and as the passage of time makes possible clearer perspective and greater objectivity, it becomes evident how complex a phenomenon it was. The underlying conditions – which did not, of course, constitute *causes* – arose from the failure of Italian liberals, during and immediately after the Risorgimento, to involve more of the population in the nation's affairs. Even as the years passed, the country's leaders were slow to move resolutely towards a broader-based political system. When greater democracy did arrive, it did so with explosive suddenness – between 1912 and 1922, when Italy was faced with the convulsive effects of war, post-war economic crises, mass demobilization, frustrated nationalism and acute social unrest. Such problems, of which social unrest was probably the most important, might have been more easily absorbed by an already established parliamentary system. It was liberal Italy's misfortune to confront acute social conflict and the arrival of the 'masses' on the political stage at the same time. Worse still, in post-war 'democratic' Italy, hundreds of thousands, perhaps millions, of Italians had no habitual or obvious political allegiance. Among them were two large and overlapping groups: war veterans, unrewarded for their sacrifices and belittled by the left; and assorted middle-class elements, some certainly conforming to De Felice's picture of a rising and ambitious class, others, especially in the countryside, more closely resembling the fearful, declining petty bourgeoisie of Marxist accounts. These Italians, attached neither to traditional liberalism, nor to political Catholicism, nor yet to socialism, comprised the mass base of the fascist movement which rose to prominence between 1920 and 1922.

Fascism obtained power not through revolution – although *threatening* revolution played a part – but as the result of Mussolini's compromise with conservative and ostensibly liberal interests. Many of Fascism's activists achieved office, status and a measure of power within the regime which subsequently emerged, but the total revolution of which some Fascists dreamed never materialized. Instead, the regime evolved into one strongly Fascist in external appearances, limited in its supposed totalitarianism by the survival of autonomous, mainly conservative forces, and distinguished by the personal power of Mussolini, its Duce. If Mussolini's regime may be said to have served the interests of his conservative allies in certain respects, this was neither deliberately and consistently intended nor necessarily bound to prove permanent. By the 1930s the decisions most liable to affect Italy's future lay in the realm of foreign policy and rested not in the hands of capitalists or militant Fascists but in those of Mussolini himself. It was those decisions, taken independently and increasingly against the wishes of his conservative fellow-travellers, that led to Mussolini's downfall and the collapse of Fascism.

The reasons for Fascism's inadequacies as a supposedly revolutionary and totalitarian regime, its military shortcomings and defeats, its decline and eventual collapse, and the personal humiliation of its leader, are not to be found in avoidable policy mistakes or errors of judgement. Rather they resulted from inherent characteristics of Fascism itself: the unfocused nature of its underlying ideas; the compromises essential for power but fatal to domestic radicalism; the susceptibility to an imperialistic expansionism that neither Fascist economic nor Fascist cultural militarism could sustain; and a leadership cult from which it could not successfully escape when the leader proved no longer worthy (assuming he ever was) of his followers' veneration.

Suggested reading

Place of publication is London unless otherwise stated.

Since Italian Fascism must be understood within the wider historical context of post-Unification Italy, a number of excellent general accounts of modern Italian history will be found useful. Two of these are relatively brief: Harry Hearder and Jonathan Morris, *Italy: A Short History* (Cambridge, Cambridge University Press, 2001) and Christopher Duggan, *A Concise History of Italy* (Cambridge, Cambridge University Press, 1994). Two longer and more detailed general histories stand out: the classic Denis Mack Smith, *Italy: A Modern History* (Ann Arbor MI, University of Michigan Press, 2nd edn, 1969) and the much more up-to-date Martin Clark, *Modern Italy 1871–1982* (Longman, 1984). Also useful is Jonathan Dunnage, *A Social History of Italy in the Twentieth Century* (Longman, 2002).

There are several good and more or less concise general treatments of Italian Fascism, of which there is room here to suggest only two: Alexander De Grand, *Italian Fascism* (Lincoln NE, University of Nebraska Press, 2nd edn, 1989) and Philip Morgan, *Italian Fascism 1915–1945* (Palgrave Macmillan, 2003). Brief overviews are provided by S.J. Woolf, 'Italy', in S.J. Woolf (ed.), *Fascism in Europe* (Methuen, 1981), pp. 39–64; Adrian Lyttelton, 'Italian Fascism', in Walter Laqueur (ed.), *Fascism. A Reader's Guide* (Wildwood House, 1976), pp. 125–50; and Roland Sarti, 'Italian fascism: radical politics and conservative goals', in Martin Blinkhorn (ed.), *Fascists and Conservatives* (Unwin

Hyman, 1990), pp. 14–30. David Forgacs (ed.), *Rethinking Italian Fascism* (Lawrence & Wishart, 1986), is an interesting collection of essays on a variety of themes. Finally, R.J.B. Bosworth's *The Italian Dictatorship: Problems and Perspectives in the Interpretation of Mussolini and Fascism* (Arnold, 1998), provides a wise and combative analysis of the historiography of Italian Fascism down almost to the end of the twentieth century.

Two important studies of Fascist ideas and ideology are Emilio Gentile, *The Origins of Fascist Ideology 1918–1925* (Enigma Books, 2005) and Zeev Sternhell *et al., The Birth of Fascist Ideology: From Cultural Revolution to Political Rebellion* (Princeton NJ, Princeton University Press, 1994); also stimulating is A. James Gregor, *Young Mussolini and the Intellectual Origins of Fascism* (Berkeley CA, University of California Press, 1979). On Fascism's foundation, its rise to power, and the early stages of the Fascist dictatorship, incomparably the best detailed study remains Adrian Lyttelton, *The Seizure of Power: Fascism in Italy, 1919–29* (Weidenfeld & Nicolson, 1973; 2nd edn, Princeton NJ, Princeton University Press, 1989). A useful and insightful contemporary account from the standpoint of Italy's democratic left is A. Rossi (a.k.a. A. Tasca), *The Rise of Italian Fascism* (New York, Gordon Press, 1976).

Several regional studies provide a sharp focus on the rise and early history of Fascism. They include Donald Bell, *Sesto San Giovanni: Workers, Culture and Politics in an Italian Town, 1880–1922* (New Brunswick NJ, Rutgers University Press, 1986); Anthony L. Cardoza, *Agrarian Elites and Italian Fascism: The Province of Bologna 1901–1926* (Princeton NJ, Princeton University Press, 1982); Paul Corner, *Fascism in Ferrara* (Oxford, Oxford University Press, 1974); Alice Kelikian, *Town and Country under Fascism: The Transformation of Brescia, 1915–26* (Oxford, Clarendon Press, 1986); Frank Snowden, *Violence and Great Estates in the South* of Italy (Cambridge, Cambridge University Press, 1986) and, by the same author, *The Fascist Revolution in Tuscany, 1919–22* (Cambridge, Cambridge University Press, 1989).

A path-breaking and thoroughly fascinating account of Italy's experience of Fascism is R.J.B. Bosworth, *Mussolini's Italy* (Penguin/ Allen Lane, 2005). Much older but still useful is Edward R. Tannenbaum, *Fascism in Italy: Society and Culture, 1922–45* (Allen Lane, 1972). Particular aspects of Italian social history under Fascism are covered in Victoria De Grazia, *The Culture of Consent: Mass Organization of Leisure in Fascist Italy* (Cambridge, Cambridge University Press, 1981) and, by the same author, *How Fascism Ruled Women. Italy 1922–1945* (Berkeley CA, University of California Press, 1992); Christopher

Duggan, *Fascism and the Mafia* (New Haven CT, Yale University Press, 1989); Tracy Koon, *Believe, Obey, Fight: Political Socialization of Youth in Fascist Italy 1922–1943* (Chapel Hill NC, University of North Carolina Press, 1985); Luisa Passerini, *Fascism in Popular Memory: The Cultural Experience of the Turin Working Class* (Cambridge, Cambridge University Press, 1987); and P.R. Willson, *The Clockwork Factory: Women and Work in Fascist Italy* (Oxford, Oxford University Press, 1993).

Fascism's relationship with big business is analysed in Roland Sarti, *Fascism and the Industrial Leadership in Italy* (Berkeley, CA, University of California Press, 1971), and that with the Vatican in D.A. Binchy, *Church and State in Fascist Italy* (Oxford University Press, 1970) and John Pollard, *The Vatican and Italian Fascism, 1929–32* (Cambridge, Cambridge University Press, 1985).

On Fascist totalitarianism, see particularly Emilio Gentile, *The Italian Road to Totalitarianism* (Routledge, 2006) and *The Sacralization of Politics in Fascist Italy* (Cambridge MA, Harvard University Press, 1996). The case for Fascism as a 'modernizing dictatorship' is made in A. James Gregor, *Italian Fascism and Developmental Dictatorship* (Princeton NJ, Princeton University Press, 1979). Three books deal with important strands within Fascism. The nationalist right is examined in Alexander De Grand, *The Italian Nationalist Association and the Rise of Fascism in Italy* (Lincoln NE, University of Nebraska Press, 1978), and the syndicalist 'left' in David D. Roberts, *The Syndicalist Tradition and Italian Fascism* (Manchester, Manchester University Press, 1979). The Fascist intelligentsia is covered in Michael Ledeen, *Universal Fascism* (New York, Howard Fertig Inc., 1972).

On foreign policy, imperialism and war, see Denis Mack Smith, *Mussolini's Roman Empire* (Penguin, 1976); G.W. Baer, *The Coming of the Italo-Ethiopian War* (Cambridge MA, Harvard University Press, 1967); Claudio Segrè, *Fourth Shore: the Italian Colonization of Libya* (Chicago IL, Universty of Chicago Press, 1988); Esmonde M. Robertson, *Mussotini as Empire-Builder: Europe and Africa, 1932–36* (Macmillan, 1977); and MacGregor Knox, *Mussolini Unleashed. Politics and Strategy in Fascist Italy's Last War* (Cambridge, Cambridge University Press, 1982). Aristotle Kallis, *Fascist Ideology: Territory and Expansionism in Italy and Germany, 1922–1945* (Routledge, 2000) explores the ideological foundations of Fascist (and Nazi) expansionism.

There are many English-language biographies of Mussolini, but three stand out. R.J.B. Bosworth, *Mussolini* (Arnold, 2002) is exceptional, but Denis Mack Smith, *Mussolini* (Granada, 1983) remains immensely valuable, while Martin Clark, *Mussolini* (Longman, 2005) is an excellent briefer alternative. It is unfortunate that Renzo De Felice's multi-volume biography has never appeared in English (even in condensed form), but at least his interpretation is available in his *Fascism: An Informal Introduction to its Theory and Practice* (New Brunswick NJ, Transaction Books, 1977). Good English-langauge biographies of other Fascist leaders are rare, but Claudio Segrè, *Italo Balbo: a Fascist Life* (Berkeley CA, University of California Press, 1988) is a distinguished exception.

On 'generic' fascism, and specifically Italian Fascism, as defined by a commitment to 'national rebirth', see Roger Griffin, *The Nature of Fascism* (Pinter, 1991). Two useful considerations of Italian Fascism within a much broader framework are Stanley G. Payne, *A History of Fascism* (Madison WI, University of Wisconsin, 1996) and *Fascism. A Comparative Approach Toward a Definition* (Madison WI, University of Wisconsin Press, 1980). Comparisons between Fascist Italy and the Nazi Third Reich are offered by R. Bessel (ed.), *Fascist Italy and Nazi Germany: Comparisons and Contrasts* (Cambridge, Cambridge University Press, 1996) and Alexander De Grand, *Fascist Italy and Nazi Germany: the 'Fascist' Style of Rule* (Cambridge, Cambridge University Press, 1995).

A number of other Lancaster Pamphlets contain material relevant to that discussed here. Important background is provided by John Gooch in *The Unification of Italy*. Italy's African interests are placed within a wider international setting in J. M. MacKenzie's *The Partition of Africa*. The general international context of Mussolini's diplomacy is presented in two pamphlets by Ruth Henig, *Versailles and After: Europe 1919–1933* and *The Origins of the Second World War*, while Mussolini's intervention in Spain is discussed in Martin Blinkhorn, *Democracy and Civil War in Spain 1931–1939*. Finally, Mussolini's fellow fascist dictator is covered in Dick Geary, *Hitler and Nazism*.

Index

Related titles from Routledge

Mussolini
3rd Edition
Peter Neville

Although he could be both ruthless and opportunistic, Benito Mussolini was also driven by ideology and his desire to make Italy great. But conservative forces in the Italian establishment and factional warfare in his own fascist party were stumbling blocks to his policy, and ultimately Italy never became as fascist as Mussolini would have liked.

Clear and engaging, this survey is key to the understanding of on f the most fascinating twentieth century European dictators.

ISBN10: 0–415–24989–9 (hb)   ISBN10: 0–415–24990– h)

ISBN13: 978–0–415–24989–8 (hb)   ISBN13: 978–0–415–24·   ⁴ (pb)

Mussolini and Fascism
Patricia Knight

The early twentieth century in Italy was a crucial period in its history. *Mussolini and Fascism* surveys all the important issues and topics of the period including the origins and rise of Fascism, Mussolini as Prime Minister and Dictator, the Totalitarian state, foreign policy and the Second World War. It also examines how Italian Fascism compared to other inter-war dictatorships.

ISBN10: 0–415–27921–6 (hb)   ISBN10: 0–415–27922–4 (pb)

ISBN13: 978–0–415–27921–5 (hb)   ISBN13: 978–0–415–27922–2 (pb)

Available at all good bookshops
For ordering and further information please visit:
www.routledge.com

Havering Sixth Form College Library

6519437